RADICAL VOICES
in the
WILDERNESS

RADICAL VOICES
in the
WILDERNESS

The Social Implications of the Prophets

Robert N. Sanders

WORD BOOKS
Waco, Texas ● London, England

Printed in the United States of America.
Library of Congress catalog card number: 74–135350

To
my sons and daughters
NEAL
LINDA
ALAN
LAURIE
whose zest for living
frees me from the
temptation of living
and preaching from
the isolation of an
ivory tower. They are,
therefore, lively words
from God to me!

CONTENTS

FOREWORD

The cliché, "Some speak because they have something to say while others speak because they have to say something," was probably composed with the preacher in mind. Sundays roll around with monotonous regularity, and the preacher is expected to make one or more appearances before his congregation every Sunday. Life being what it is, the preacher does not come to his pulpit each time with the same high level of emotional stimulation and mental preparation. There are times, to be sure, when everything is right. The spokesman for God has left no aspect of preparation undone. "He has something to say," and he is constrained to say it. On the other hand, even the most able preachers have their dry spells. The Sunday morning appearance during such times becomes a struggle for the preacher and a burden for his congregation. "The preacher has to say something." He is constrained by the occasion. And the congregation's reaction gives substance to the taunt, "Ignore him! He is just preaching!"

We live in the midst of a revolution. This is (or should be) the preacher's finest hour. The people are hungry for an authentic word but they cannot and will not endure the pummelings of one who is "just preaching." The preacher must go hard if he would be informed in the highly technical world of today, and he must work hard if he would offer a compelling word in a world agitated by revolutionary forces.

Analogies to the modern preacher's situation in life abound in the history of the people of God. The times of the great prophets of Israel, of Jesus and the apostles, and of the church from the sub-apostolic period until Constantine have points of contact with our era. The people of God survived those bitter times scathed and scarred but full of hope because there were men of insight and prophetic skill who charged the people to be what they were meant to be—the people of God! These men of God had something worth saying and they said it.

The role of the people of God today is what it has always been, and that is to *be* the people of God. The word "church" originally meant "that which belongs to the Lord." The preacher's task is to charge the people to assume their role. It is by denotation a servant's role, for "that which belongs to the Lord" exists solely to serve the Lord. This is one strand which went into the making of this book. What R. N. Sanders has to say is a forthright and courageous appeal to the church to be itself, the servant of the Lord.

Another of these strands is that men do not write books for precisely the same reasons that they preach sermons. The latter task is much less painstaking and considerably less difficult. I would like to believe that men write books because they have something to say, but Ecclesiastes refuted that argument before it was conceived.

Perhaps it happens that a man writes a book simply because he feels that he has something worth sharing and the printed page seems to be his medium. This in itself is reason enough! Every man has a right to his day. . . . he should not —and if America is to stand as a nation of free people, must not—be shouted down before he is heard. This is the plea I would make for this book: *know for sure what it says before you cast it aside.* I am certain that this is all that its author would ask.

This book did not come easily. It has a life of agonizing study, painful introspection, and courageous experimentation behind it. Whatever it may lack, it does not lack genuineness. It is for real! Like all books, this one has its presuppositions. Unlike many books, these presuppositions are not camouflaged. Herein is its major strength, and on this basis the book's worth should be judged.

Without preempting the author's message, a few of his most salient assumptions may be mentioned. The author assumes (1) that the church and her spokesmen have gotten us off the track and that only the church and her spokesmen can get us back on the track again. The author assumes that (2) biblical literalism (euphemism for "bibliolatry"), pietistic individualism (my "soul" is saved), the church's aversion to the social dimension of the gospel at the grass-roots level, and the church's narcissistic obsession with "plants" and "programs" (perfect attendance buttons, etc.) are millstones around her neck that have pulled her down to something worse than death, i.e., a bastion of defense for the status quo. The author assumes (3) that the Bible rightly understood has a live word for us that will both shock and heal. The author assumes (4) that the message of the Bible can and must be made relevant in an age whose world view, line of reasoning and style of life have opened up an identity gap—the gap between who we are and who we could be. We have been men dedicated to forging and using instruments of war; we could be men dedicated to making peace. We have been exclusivist men hardened by prejudice and racism; we could be inclusivist men dedicated to the gospel of enlightenment and love.

This book may not—probably cannot—stem the tide which at this very moment seems to be sweeping us over the precipice. It will, however, enable the one to "run that readeth it." It is a prophetic word in the best sense of the term. It is given, I am sure, with the hope that it is not too late!

HARRY E. MOORE, JR.
Nashville, Tennessee

PREFACE

Several events converged on me to bring this book into being. The first was my casual encounter, while browsing in a bookstore, with J. Elliott Corbett's paperback *The Prophets On Main Street*. By his creative and imaginative interpretation of five Old Testament prophets, the prophets spoke to me in a way that they had not previously.

The second was a decision to begin a series of sermons on the prophets in my own pulpit in the First Baptist Church of Lewisburg, Tennessee. I wanted to present the compelling social message of the prophets—what was needed was for these ancient writings to speak in contemporary language to a contemporary congregation in relation to contemporary issues.

The third event was the appearance of W. R. Rogers in Nashville and Middle Tennessee to promote his candidacy for the presidency of the United States (see chapter 1 for further amplification).

The fourth event was the reception which these sermons received when first delivered from my pulpit. They were greeted with some misunderstanding, with blatant hostility, and with total indifference. They were also greeted positively by several people; some were awakened to a new understanding of prophetic religion; the sensitivity of others to social issues was sharpened; and some renewed their commitment to struggle personally for the elimination of social inequities. On the whole, however, the sermons were not received with overwhelming enthusiasm; rather, they created discussion and conflict. But agreement or disagreement was not the intended goal, only understanding of and insight into prophetic religion. By the time the first four or five had been preached, I was certain that they were a needed corrective for a congregation whose corporate worship life had been a bland diet consisting of a "cake not turned." At this point, with the encouragement of some friends, I decided to make these sermons available in print.

I had thought of titling this book *Conscripts of Conscience*, seeking to convey something of the intense sense of divine compulsion that moved these prophets to challenge the entrenched social ills of their day. In their own ways, loyal to whatever insight into justice was theirs and acting on the basis of their understanding of God, these prophets flung down the gauntlet of challenge before the rampant inequities of their time.

St. Paul, centuries later, defined himself as a "bond-slave" of the gospel. The prophets, too, felt themselves to be slaves, conscripted to preach. It was a sense of urgency which moved them to deliver themselves of the overwhelming burdens that plagued their consciences. They were conscience-stricken over the injustices of their day, the exploitation of the poor and the abuse of the disinherited. They were burdened with an agonizing sensitivity and an authentic concern for the oppressed.

In no sense, however, were they threatened into obedience; rather, they were captivated into obeying the moral constraints which were placed on them by their consciences. And as "conscripts of conscience" they could not but call men to a radical obedience of God's austere demand for justice.

I am prepared for the fact that some controversy may arise over several areas of this book. Some may try to dismiss the book as the mere protest of an "angry young Turk." Admittedly, there are some places where my commitment to, zeal for, and exuberance over my understanding of the gospel contributes to an over-statement of the case. This I confess, but for it I offer no apology. I can truthfully say that I am not interested in being politely ignored. I am prepared for the anguish that can come. The chapters in this book unswervingly pursue my understanding of and commitment to the gospel; therefore, I do not want to risk being so ambiguous that I am understood in any direction or so evasive that no hard issues are faced. I view this book as the attempt of an honest pastor to help his denomination and the church face the twentieth century and its issues with candor and realism. The issues which are raised in this book are holding the attention of a major segment of the Christian world. Whatever relevance and meaning there is to be found in this book is related to the heritage from which this book has emerged and to which it seeks to speak.

It will be obvious to anyone who reads this book that I have drawn heavily from many sources. For example, the chronology of John Paterson's book *The Goodly Fellowship of the Prophets* was accepted as plausible and reasonable. With only minor divergences from his chronology I have sought to set each prophetic oracle in its historical framework and have arranged them in that chronological order throughout.

Moreover, I have carefully documented the points at which I recognize and remember my debt to others. I hope that the places where I have "conveniently" forgotten my debt to others will convey my gratitude by the sympathetic nature with which the passage is treated. I am grateful for permission to quote from their works extended by authors and publishers. I have sought to convey that thanks throughout the manuscript in the footnotes.

Mr. Floyd W. Thatcher, Senior Editor of Word Books, has given professional assistance to me in bringing this venture to its climax. I want to express my personal gratitude to him for his incisive insight into areas that eluded me. I would express my appreciation to Miss Frances Hill, secretary of the First Baptist Church, Lewisburg, Tennessee, for her willingness to assume responsibility for a second manuscript when previous experience had been her pedagogue that the task is demanding.

The Foreword is written by my friend the Rev. Harry E. Moore, Jr., of Nashville, Tennessee. He has given of himself unstintingly at numerous times in the final drafting of these pages. Several of his suggestions have been embodied into this book, and it is the stronger for them. When his suggestions have not been taken literally they have, at least, been taken seriously. He, therefore, joins me in seeking to make this book a lively, communicative word from God for our day.

1. INTRODUCTION

The Prophet on the Court Square

During the summer of 1967 a man named Bishop W. R. Rogers frequented several of the cities of Tennessee. He identified himself as the presidential candidate of the Theocratic Party. He was traveling around the country in order to dramatize his candidacy for the presidency of the United States. To accomplish this purpose he was assuming a role similar to that of the biblical Joshua. His Jericho was the courthouse, and the wall shutting him out was iniquity in government. By making seven Joshuaic jaunts around the courthouse he was, symbolically at least, challenging that iniquity. At the conclusion of the seventh lap a defiant blast on his trumpet was to bring about a shattering downfall similar to the fate which befell Jericho of antiquity.

If the people reacted as I suspect they did and as, admittedly, I did, then they wrote him off as a harmless and innocuous quack. I smiled and dismissed his buffoonery as the cheap antics of a man who was starved for public attention. I did so, that is, until I began to write this introduction to my projected series of sermons on the social implications of the Old Testament prophets. And the more I reflected on Rogers' comical stance and his self-righteous claim to be a serious presidential candidate, the more I came to realize that the public had been exposed to the same kind of drama as that in which the Old Testament prophets had clothed their ministry and message. Here was a man who was tolerated by the public with good-natured humor because he was, obviously, harmless and irrelevant to the raw realities of the political arena from which candidates were actually thrust into the campaign for the office at the head of the government of the United States of America. Yet, even though this was the case, he was heard. This man called attention to himself and his message because he dared to assume the role of a "prophet on the court square."

Lest I be misunderstood, I should say that I do not believe that Bishop Rogers was a prophet. Moreover, I am not suggesting that a twentieth-century prophet must assume the role of a public clown in order to gain a hearing. Furthermore, I do not believe his contention that our public officials in government are unusually iniquitous. Although it is a popular claim in some quarters to maintain that the members of the Supreme Court are communist sympathizers or, at the very least, dupes of the communist conspiracy, that the Congress is composed of ill-informed men whose major interest is in their own personal profit and political careers, that Washington is faithless in administering the will of the majority, and that politicians are corrupt men who know little about personal integrity, I do not believe that this is the case in any major sense. Actually, men in government are no worse than the average citizen of our country. And, in many cases, their basic integrity and sensitivity supercedes the self-righteous claim of many of their most vocal critics. Bishop Rogers was just playing the leading role in a circuitous melodrama.

But the point which kept coming back to plague my mind was that here was an individual whose comic opera role reflected the Old Testament portrayal of an ancient prophet! Obviously we need to understand the prophet of the Old Testament and the role which biblical, prophetic preaching plays in a modern church. There is a genuine need for that prophetic voice to be heard calling men back to social justice, to personal integrity, and to a respect for the person in a universal community of humanity. Indeed, it is true that

> in the goodly fellowship of the prophets we meet with a religious phenomenon unique and without parallel. Here we have to deal with one of the profound movements of the human spirit and with the most significant aspect of Old Testament revelation. Prophets there have been in other religions and in other times, but nowhere do we find a comparable succession of mighty creative personalities who linked the prophetic impulse to spiritual religion and made the religion of Israel a permanent force in the world and a real preparation for the Christian Gospel.[1]

Therefore, it is my hope that these prophets will speak again. Originally, they spoke in the peculiar idiom of their own day. I want to recover the incisive thrust of their messages, to recapture the essential heart of their burdens, and to address their oracles to sophisticated and secular America, to the disciple whose vocational life forces him to take his pilgrimage into a world that, increasingly, is moving away from God. It is my hope that these prophets will steel us for our trek into the heart of the secular city, so that through us the prophetic voice will be heard challenging a world come of age. This task demands courageous audacity and the gallant-hearted serenity of a life totally open to God, so that he may move in us and through us toward the healing of the wounds, pains, and pangs of a fragmented, distraught humanity.

I. The Prophetic Ministry

A prophet is a man who "stands between God and man with the responsibility of faithfully declaring to man what he has heard from God." He has "an ear open continually toward God to hear what he has to say to weary, broken, stumbling humanity," who has "a tongue ready and disciplined to speak the cauterizing and healing words" [2] of God. In the Old Testament he is understood as a man who has no

---

1. John Paterson, *The Goodly Fellowship of the Prophets* (New York: Scribner's, 1950), p. 1.

2. James D. Smart, *The Rebirth of Ministry* (Philadelphia: Westminster, 1960), pp. 54–55.

option but to speak, whose word bears the authenticating preface, "thus saith the Lord," whose burden is given divine sanction by the seal "this is the oracle of the Lord." Thus, the prophet speaks for God to the times in which he lives.

It should be noted that this understanding of the function of a prophet is rooted in the biblical meaning of the word for prophet. It does not mean soothsayer or fortuneteller. The prophet is not someone with a crystal ball from deity who, by virtue of his divine gift, predicts future events. Those who suppose the Old Testament prophets to be mere prognosticators who spent all their time predicting the future have a mistaken notion of the prophet's role. He was a man who stood within the historical framework of his own day and time and spoke for God by seeking to interpret the divine will to men.

Moreover, the prophet understands the ultimate implications of his preaching. John Skinner asserts that the prophets "appear to have been endowed with remarkable insight into the providential significance of the political events of their time." [3] The primary task of the prophet is to speak for God in a given historical context and situation. It is this precise involvement in the present that leads him to conclusions with implications for the future. Therefore, it is not totally accurate to describe the prophet as a spokesman of God so immersed in the swift-moving tide of the present that he never addresses himself to the future.

The prophet who accepts the responsibility of speaking for God to his own day is assuming an awesome and demanding task. It is awesome in that it is presumptuous to speak to men for God. And the only way to avoid that task becoming a cardinal presumption is for the prophet to keep always in mind that he is only the personality through whom God speaks. He must never resolve the tension of such a task by assuming an infallible stance. To do so is to presume himself indispensable. On the other hand, he must not resolve the

---

3. John Skinner, *Prophecy and Religion* (Cambridge: University Press, 1951), p. 7.

tension by such overwhelming self-effacement that he refuses to immerse himself in the historical self-revelation of God through his dealings with Israel. Either imbalance can become a perversion of the prophetic utterance. He must remember that the open encounter of divergent convictions can lead to the discovery of the deeper implications of the gospel.

The task is demanding in that it is a dual role which the prophet is called to fulfill. The role is a negative one of judgment, and it is a positive one of the promise of hope and redemption and healing. The negative role is a responsibility to prick people's consciences about those evils and disorders in the world which stem from a ruptured relationship between God and man. "The prophet is needed most at the very point where self-deception has been most destructive, where people have developed a shell to protect some privilege, some vested interest, some special source of pride, some favorite dogma, some idol of the spirit. The prophet speaks for God, who judges everything human, the ideals and achievements of every society, especially all that is proud and lofty, all that is high and lifted up. He speaks for God, who is concerned for the victims of the pride, the greed, and the blindness of men." [4]

This negative role is described in one of the novels of the British writer and poet George MacDonald. In *The Marquis of Lossie* he writes of the preaching of a schoolmaster. "To those who understood, it was as if he would force his way through every stockade of prejudice, ditch of habit, rampart of indifference, moat of sin, wall of stupidity, and curtain of ignorance, until he stood face to face with the conscience of his hearers." [5]

On the positive side, the prophet is a voice calling for the restoration of the fragmented relationship between creature and Creator. He calls for social justice where there is only injustice and discrimination, for personal integrity where there is only a denial of the values inherent in persons, and

4. John C. Bennett, "The Prophetic Side of Christianity," *Best Sermons, 1955* (New York: McGraw-Hill, 1955), pp. 278–79.

5. Quoted by Henry Sloane Coffin in "Preaching in an Age of Disillusionment," *Best Sermons, 1947–48* (New York: Harper and Brothers, 1948), p. xiv.

for peace among men where there is only bitterness, hatred and strife. He speaks of the abiding dream wherein social justice is the only acceptable adhesive holding together the institutional structures of a society. He speaks of the glowing hope wherein personal integrity is the reality of the day. He speaks of the gleaming vision wherein peace is the discovery and recovery of the wholeness of life's adventure.

II. The Prophetic Role of Jesus

In the light of the demanding nature of the prophetic role, it is significant that Jesus accepted this role when he made the momentous decision about his ministry. In his temptation in the wilderness, three shadowy silhouettes were vying for his eternal commitment. He was wrestling with the question of "what kind of a Messiah shall I be? Shall I yield to the popular expectations and be a bread-giving, wonder-working, enemy-conquering Messiah, or shall I be some other kind of Messiah?" He asked himself, "Shall I take the easy road of expediency and compromise or shall I take the hard road of absolute obedience to my Father's voice and my Father's will, even though that road may lead to a cross? Since I am the Son of God, there is no reason for me to have to suffer; I can make bread from these stones! Is this the way for me?" The lucid preacher Paul Scherer expressed the struggle in these words:

> Is that a dead end, a blind alley, a pitiful surrender, a grave for all your bright hopes, with the heavy earth falling? It's God's way of winning! It's the victory over us that's for us. It's God bringing the issue as near the level of his love as his power can lift it! Satan whispered, and the crowd shouted, "If you are the Son of God, don't just stand there, do something!" Maybe we should turn it wrong side out! "If you are the Son of God, don't just do something! Stand there, in my sorrow and loneliness, in all my frustration and defeat, where the shadows are—until the day breaks, as thou wilt have it break, and thy grace makes my weakness strength!" [6]

---

6. Paul Scherer, *The Word God Sent* (New York: Harper and Brothers, 1965), pp. 151–52.

It was the same struggle which climaxed with the classic words, "Father, if you will, take this cup away from me. Not my will, however, but your will be done." To take the way of radical obedience to the will of God is to enfold one's self in the role of the Old Testament prophet.

In the struggle of his soul, Jesus' prophetic ministry was shaped and molded by another facet of his decision. Jesus was tempted to throw himself from the pinnacle of the Temple and "set men aghast by such a feat. But He rejected investing his life in this way and took on that more awesome task of trying to bring men to wholeness rather than simply bringing them to their feet in applause." [7] This was to reject what F. W. Dillistone calls "playing to the gallery." Jesus "refused to purchase the plaudits of the crowd at the cost of toying with triviality. He would die rather than make a convenience or a cheap advertisement of the power and providence of God." [8] This kind of inner integrity is essential if one is to be committed to a prophetic ministry with rectitude.

The third facet of Jesus' struggle was the temptation to force the issue, as Dillistone has suggested. Can I force people to an acceptance of God's kingdom since it is for their good? Can I regiment people into the kingdom of God? Can I force the kingdom on men? Can I demand blind servitude? These were the questions with which Jesus was wrestling. Judas succumbed to the easy way—he would have answered "yes" to these questions. His action was more an attempt to force Jesus into this understanding of his ministry than it was an utter treasonous betrayal of a friend.

Jesus recognized that this was a temptation to violate persons rather than to let them mature in responsible freedom. Forcing and regimenting would deny his unswerving fidelity to the inherent and inviolable dignity of persons. This commitment to persons was the radical dimension of his ministry. His struggle with this temptation promised no easy victory.

---

7. From a sermon by John R. Claypool and used with his permission.

8. F. W. Dillistone, *Jesus Christ and His Cross* (Philadelphia: Westminster, 1953), p. 24.

By choosing the path of an uncompromising commitment to the integrity of persons, Jesus was taking upon himself the harsh and demanding heritage bequeathed through the Old Testament prophets.

In Jesus' life and ministry the prophetic heritage came to its most intense focus. Jesus' ministry had a social dimension steeped in the rich tradition of the Old Testament prophets. He demonstrated a compassionate concern for persons in all that he did. He spoke fearlessly to his age and called it "an evil and adulterous generation." He sternly denounced those whose only concern was for the theological precision of a dogma, for tithing mint and dill and cummin while neglecting justice and mercy and love. His denunciation of the social ills of his day was so scathing and complete that he announced, "I tell you that the publicans and harlots will march into heaven ahead of you"—you who claim to be working in God's vineyard when it is obvious you are not.

III. The Prophetic Heritage of the Minister

In today's world the minister has been bequeathed the heritage of the biblical, prophetic tradition. Genuinely to enter into this heritage is to enter a path fraught with dangers and pitfalls. Some people do not want a minister to be faithful to the proclamation of the whole counsel of God. A prophet whose sole authority is God is called to declare "idolatrous and blasphemous all modes of life and trends of thought that confound the created and the Creator." It was Ferré who expressed it in this manner,

> Prophetic preaching denounces all traditionalism and conservatism that would keep God's fresh light from breaking through, showing the darkness of man's previous worship, however hallowed it has been held to be. Biblicism, moralism, ecclesiasticism —all human ways of stifling true worship—are flayed by the prophet who stands within God's new anger against the evil past of the church. The prophet of the new day dares not linger in the shadows of the dark past.[9]

---

9. Nels F. S. Ferré, "The Place of Preaching in the Modern World," *The Pulpit,* December, 1962, pp. 7–8.

This is a message which many ears find difficult to heed. They do not care for a minister whose preaching threatens their structured vested interests. If he challenges their complacency, rebukes their prejudice, and rejects the claims of the Establishment to be sole possessors of righteous concern for the dispossessed, he is not appreciated, regardless of how closely his prophetic preaching parallels that of the Old Testament prophets. The people whose guilt marshals itself disguised as prudence will manufacture a defense.

Such a defense has been given vocal expression by J. Howard Pew, the chairman of the board of Sun Oil Company. He contends that "statecraft or economics" are secular areas outside the jurisdiction of the church and consequently of the minister. He clarifies what he means by "statecraft or economics" with his statement that the church is

> . . . leaping headlong into such fundamentally secular concerns as federal aid to education, civil rights, urban renewal, the nation's foreign policy, and plugging for such controversial issues as the admission of Red China to the United Nations, disarmament, higher minimum wages, forcible union membership, etc.[10]

Granting the responsibility of the individual Christian to express his convictions in economic, social and political affairs, he would deny the corporate church a right to voice its concern for areas of life to which the Old Testament prophets spoke.

Such a theory as his would emasculate the minister, render the church impotent and completely irrelevant to the issues of the day, and jettison the biblical understanding of the prophetic role. It is this very real attempt to silence the prophetic voice of the church, coupled I might add with the church's acquiescence in many places, that has caused so many perceptive voices to suggest that the day of the institutional church is passed and to clamor for a "religionless Christianity." But Dag Hammarskjöld was right when he asserted in his journal, "In our era, the road to holiness passes

---

10. J. Howard Pew, "Should the Church 'Meddle' in Civil Affairs?" *Readers' Digest*, May, 1966.

through the world of action." [11] This is just as true for the church as it is for the individual.

The voice of "the prophet on the court square," the man of God totally immersed and involved in the thick of life,[12] is in some danger in our day of being stifled and snuffed out by friends of the church. To use the title of Pierre Berton's book, many friends of the church refuse to hear the prophetic voice because what they desire is "the comfortable pew."

And this happens for many reasons.[13] Many who occupy the pews want them to be a comfortable interlude in the midst of the wild melee called life. And prophets have an annoying way of making a pew uncomfortable. They are not content to preach an anemic and pale imitation of the demanding rigor of the gospel. They are always striking out at that self-righteous smugness and inordinate self-concern that is so characteristic of an Elder Brother. When there is a demand from the pew that the prophet pronounce woes against the Detroit rioters, the prophet refuses to give that kind of comfort at the expense of getting to the real heart of the matter. He refuses to treat cancerous pride with the application of a band-aid, but denounces those conditions which make rioting easy to justify by rationalization.

No one can deny that much life in the inner city seems little worse than hell! The prophet condemns the slum conditions presided over by wealthy and compassionless lords. He lays the fault at the feet of an affluent society indifferent to abject poverty. His prophetic burden is against a society which is so highly industrialized that it produces the overwhelming bulk of the world's automobiles, telephones and appliances, yet has so much unemployment. He condemns the kind of discrimination which is so much a part of the American cultural fabric—even though open housing is the law of the land it is an illusive dream for many rather than a

11. Dag Hammarskjöld, Markings (New York: Alfred A. Knopf, 1965), p. 122.

12. There is a spirited editorial by Samuel McCrea Cavert in Pulpit Digest, June, 1965, contending for this very involvement.

13. These emphases were suggested by Alfred McBride's "How To Tell A Real Prophet," The Pulpit, January 1966, pp. 18–19.

present reality. Only after exposing and denouncing the root causes does the prophet turn to condemn rioting, looting, and murder. Yet even with the destruction resulting from such action there is still a hard core of resistance to the war on poverty which seeks to uproot the presiding causes from their slum empires.

Too many people in the church seek to stifle the prophetic voice because they are blind to that elusive quality of life which beckons us ever onward. But the prophet envisions that quality of life, clamors for their openness to it, and seeks to move the people of God toward that new day. His understanding of his role circumvents any easy temptation to pattern his ministry into an acceptable and more popular form. Easy platitudes offer no escape for him. He must announce the reality of God's new age. Rooted in his own day he sees the world as God means it to be in terms of his universal kingdom. He sees the diametrical cleavage between the kind of world in which he lives and the world as it must become in God's new age. "He transcends time and lives in the eternal now of God's victory." [14] Blindness to this understanding of the prophetic task which tries to silence the prophet in today's church is really trying to avoid the fierce light of God's truth.

Therefore, the minister who seeks to be a "prophet on the court square," immersed in the swift-moving stream of life, must seek to help men grapple with the contradictions of the time. He must invade that moving tide of history with a clear and live word from God. He must challenge life's dark riddle with imaginative and courageous delight. He must challenge a compassionless society. He must throw open life to those breathtaking demands which are part of being the church in a modern society.

So the prophetic voice is to be raised again in this twentieth century, on the court square. It is the prophetic voice which calls, clearly and resonantly, "Why, O America, are you so arrogant and vain? Have you forgotten that it was the Lord God who delivered you from the impending Nazi slav-

---

14. Ferré, *op. cit.*, p. 8.

ery and gave to you a land spared the scars of battle? The day is upon you," the prophet continues, "when the world will rise up against you with a single voice. Woe to those who are at ease in America for I shall visit you, says the Lord, with those same inhumanities of which you are guilty, and I shall permit the same proportion of violence to be meted out against you which you have meted out against the nations!" In the name of the Lord, the prophet reminds us that no land or nation can survive which permits injustice upon its people.

"Another John the Baptist shall haunt your vacation wonderlands with the piercing call for national and individual repentance. Those cities of men which you are seeking to make the citadels of your secular kingdoms shall become the cities of your captivity. Those cities wherein poverty reigns shall be brought low."

The prophetic voice of Jesus must be raised on the court squares. Jesus was not only a gentle man of healing balm and redeeming grace. He called for the surrender of the totality of life. He condemned those callous hearts which are insensitive to human hurt. He condemned those who cluck their tongues so disapprovingly of rioting while their inner lives are cruel, hard, and sterile. He condemned all of the inhumanity which is so much a part of our land.

So these ancient prophets must speak again, and they will if we will but open our deaf ears to whatever they shall say. And there is one thing of which we may be certain. If the prophets of the Old Testament were to be heard candidly and honestly, there would not be a chance for us to rest and relax unperturbed. Their scathing words would pierce our indifference and be the live, jolting, unsettling words of God for our day!

2. AMOS

Religion Without Righteousness

Scripture: Amos 2:6, 7a; 5:21–24

Late in 1967 Bishop Horace Donegan, Episcopal Bishop of New York, announced that the Cathedral of St. John the Divine would remain unfinished and would stand as a symbol of the anguish and the unrelieved despair of the disadvantaged millions of people in the ghettos of the city. It is to stand unfinished "until there is greater evidence that the despair and anguish of our unadvantaged people has been relieved. The unfinished cathedral shall be the prophetic symbol that our society is still rough-hewn, ragged, broken and incomplete as the building itself."

As the prophet Amos moved through the cities of Israel in the eighth century before Christ, he saw that society was "rough–hewn, ragged, broken and incomplete." He had come from his home in the wilderness of Tekoa, a barren and bleak area south of Jerusalem, to the markets of the north. He eked out an existence as a shepherd and as a dresser of a variety of fig—his task was to cut open the top of each fig to ensure and hasten its ripening. Marketing his fruit and wool took him to the trading centers of Bethel, Gilgal, Gaza, Samaria, and Damascus. In each of the cities he observed that the society of his day was plagued with injustice toward the dispossessed and with the exploitation of the poor. The poor were harried

29

by day and haunted by night because of their debts. The rich had no concern for the oppressed; the poor were so completely at the mercy of the wealthy that they were often sold into slavery to pay for their debts. The courts had been corrupted by bribes so that justice was out of reach of any except the rich.

Amos was overwhelmed by the abuse and exploitation of human beings in these cities. On the other side of the gulf between the haves and the have-nots lived those for whom security and status, evidenced by their summer homes decorated with ivory and gold, were of more consequence than human welfare. Everywhere Amos saw evidence of this cleavage between those who lived in opulence and idleness and those shackled by the chains of poverty.

In spite of these abuses, national life was permeated with a mood of optimism and confidence. The serenity and peace of the forty years of Jeroboam II's reign was helping to create the unparalleled affluence. His reign, which had begun at the time when Assyria defeated Syria, spread its influence across much of the known world and expanded Israel's dominion over numerous surrounding territories. Such a time of peace and affluence permitted luxury to flourish. Society, then, was characterized by its contrasts.

Religion was just another facet of the general outlook. In Israel the people felt that they were the favored worshipers of a very powerful God. They were fastidiously zealous in their worship of this obliging deity. They established elaborate feast days and offered sacrifices to insure God's continuing participation in their prosperity. National survival, personal security, success, and God—the four were as synonymous in ancient Israel as they are today. So Amos was moving among a people who were religious. It was a religion without righteousness, a cultus without compassion and concern. The Israelites' understanding of God and their relationship to him had no connection with justice for the oppressed, healing for the disinherited who were bleeding and suffering, or freedom for those imprisoned in society's ghettos.

But that which troubled Amos the most was the silence of

the prophetic voice. The only voices being heard were those which baptized the cultural mores into acceptable society with an unctuous permissiveness and tolerance of social evil. They tried to cover the emptiness of their message by using the proper ecclesiastical and theological terms, and pious but meaningless platitudes and shibboleths. The prophets had sold their souls for acceptance and security. They had forfeited their right to speak the words of God to man in return for the secure position of chaplains of the Establishment.

Into this scene strode a rugged, courageous shepherd to expose a false religion which put ritual above righteousness, the cultus above compassion, and status above justice. Amos had not succumbed to the kind of schizophrenic religion that seeks to drive a wedge between personal righteousness and involvement in the amelioration of social ills. He had never been stopped by the kind of claim or assertion which Clarence B. Randall makes in his book *Freedom's Faith*—that "religion is meaningful and holy because it stands serenely above all controversy."

Amos's task was to bring back to meaningful, vital faith a people who had accepted spurious substitutes. Their sensitivity to evil, sin, and suffering had atrophied. Amos's experience in the cities of Israel had opened his eyes to the anguish suffered by the downtrodden, and he was determined to set God's healing grace against Israel's betrayal of her role as the people of God. The brutality of her citizens was a sin against the moral nature of God.

Amos began his message with the call of God which he pictured as echoing over all the land of Israel. Then he turned his attention to the enemies of Israel. They had violated international treaties, defied the moral structures of the nations, and destroyed the mutual trust and good will of neighboring peoples. They had abused human life, created an insurmountable barrier of hatred among the nations and shackled humanity with a heritage of militarism. They must all stand before the wrath of a righteous God, warned Amos. Then he moved to an indictment of Judah, Israel's sister kingdom to the south. Although the Temple of God was in

Judah, she had rejected God's law and had violated God's ethical justice and moral order.

But the real target of Amos was Israel. He pronounced her guilty of creating woe and hurt and bereavement by her treatment of the poor and her love of luxury. The atrocities perpetuated by the people of Israel on their own poor brothers were as terrible as the atrocities of war. They were no better than the nations of the world community who did not worship God. They were guilty of oppressing the poor! Guilty of crushing the needy! Guilty of bartering human life for the settlement of debts! Guilty of indolence and indifference to pain and suffering.

I. Identification with the Dispossessed

Amos's prophetic burden was directed toward that kind of religion which is no longer able to identify with the weak, the poor, and the dispossessed. In Israel, the prophets had sold out for security and had thereby lost their sensitivity to the ills and inequities of the social structures of their land. In their struggle to save their life they had lost it and their souls. They had bartered with the power structure only to become identified with it. They had lost contact with those sources of power and strength, warmth and concern which used to remind them of the burden of a suffering people.

The live word of God surges out of Amos's writings [1] at this very point. During the period following World War II when the church was struggling with its imperatives to

---

1. Some scholars believe that the Old Testament book identified by the title *Amos* was not actually given written form by the prophet Amos. They contend that literary criticism reveals his oracles to have had an oral history, a development through at least two written collections of his sayings, a wedding of the oracle collection (1:3–2:3, 2:6–16, 3:2–8, 3:9–4:3, 4:4–6:14) with the vision collection (7:1–9, 8:1–2, 9:1) and some final additions (4:13, 5:8–9, 9:5–6) by some copyist. This is not to weaken the significance of Amos; rather, it strengthens the book by contending that there was a group of sensitive Hebrews who were able to recognize truth and who were seeking to preserve it for posterity. Throughout this sermon, then, the words "Amos's writings" refer to that group of prophetic utterances collected under the name of the prophet Amos. See George A. Buttrick, ed., *The Interpreter's Dictionary of the Bible* (New York: Abingdon, 1962), pp. 116–21, for full account of this viewpoint.

preach the gospel to the whole world, it chose the way of ministering to those who dominate and influence society. The church learned to communicate with those whose decisions mold the structures of society. Such a choice forced the church to forfeit its identification with those who do not have the power to structure society. In its drive for acceptance, security, financial strength and influence, the church chose to identify itself with those status groups of the power structure who detest social change. Acceptance has been purchased at the price of soul and conscience. A dulled social conscience and an openness to the needy forfeited—this is the price of security and acceptance. The struggle of the church in this decade is the concerted attempt to buy back its tainted soul. But although the church knows the way of communicating with the power structure, it has few avenues left to communicate its concern to the children of God in the direst need!

The concern for renewal of the church is, in part, the struggle for devising and discovering ways to communicate the gospel of acceptance, love, forgiveness and fulfillment to those who no longer care to listen because they were shut out and pushed aside at the time of their deepest need. Those who were shunned in a time of pragmatic choice have turned a deaf ear to the gospel.

Moreover, this attempt at renewal is complicated by the fact that the church is slow to transform its noble affirmations of justice into practical acts of mercy. Many who mouth pious platitudes of brotherhood, racial justice, and international peace and good will are content merely to affirm them from lofty and safe pulpits; in the asphalt jungles of the secular city they would deny to some of God's unfortunate children what they affirm to be those people's inalienable rights as the result of their creation in God's image.

The church has forgotten the aim of its existence. While the world is in the throes of revolution, while the disinherited are struggling for decent housing, for equality of job opportunity, and for racial equality, the church is only going through the motions of concern, squeaking out its words of good cheer. The harsh word of Amos to the church is that the measure of corporate vitality as of personal religious vitality is always identification with those in need. The concerned Christian in the 1970s will seek ways to identify with the disinherited, not because they are good but because they are downtrodden. He will seek ways to identify with minority groups, not because they are better than anyone else but because they are plagued with inner fears and outer resentments. He will identify with those who are estranged, not because they are clever but because they are alone. He will identify with the socially and economically deprived, not because they are grateful for help but because they are hurt. When a Christian is seeking to live what Bultmann called an "authentic existence" he will identify with the weak, the poor, and the disenfranchised.

What I mean is illustrated by a poignant incident related in Elizabeth Yates's book *Howard Thurman: Portrait of a Practical Dreamer*. When Howard Thurman was in India in 1935, he spoke in many villages. Late one night a lad knocked on his door. His dress revealed that he was an "untouchable," and he told his story in broken, faltering English. "I stood outside the building and listened to your lecture, Sahib Doctor. Tell me, please, can you give some hope to a nobody?" The boy fell to his knees and Thurman reached out compassionately to him. Thurman knew what it is to be classed as a "nobody." He had committed his life to the ministry of a love that identifies with suffering humanity, of reaching out to "nobodies." And Amos is incontestably clear that authentic religious experience moves one compassionately to identify with anyone in need.

II. Alleviation of Humanity's Hurt

Amos bluntly condemned Israel for the injustices and inequities of society. But, more than this, he insisted that religion must be concerned with the social conditions that strangle men.

The Christian church cannot live out its life in isolation

from the agonies and struggles of men. It is deceitful to claim that the God of the church "desires all men to be saved and to come to the knowledge of the truth"[2] while its adherents remain aloof from humanity's hurt. Moreover, it is hypocritical to try to identify with people while refusing to become involved in trying to eradicate the evil dimensions of their environment. To be content with personal piety and morality, to be obsessed with creedal rectitude and correct theology while refusing to deal with the ghetto lords who profit from the misery of slum rentals, is a dichotomy which Amos condemned! The church cannot tolerate evil, regardless of the risk of its involvement in correcting abuses. It is the business of the church to "preach the Good News to the poor, to proclaim liberty to the captives, to set free the oppressed." It is the business of the church to speak an abrasive word of God to any social condition that shackles men. Yes, the extent to which the church "witnesses more courageously, prays more faithfully, believes more joyously and loves more ardently" in its private discipline and through its corporate witness determines the extent to which the church is church.

That prophet of the twentieth century, Martin Luther King, Jr., put the thought in incisive words.

The church must be reminded that it is not the master or the servant of the state, but rather the conscience of the state. It must be the guide and the critic of the state, and never its tool. If the church does not recapture its prophetic zeal, it will become an irrelevant social club without moral or spiritual authority. If the church does not participate actively in the struggle for peace and for economic and racial justice, it will forfeit the loyalty of millions and cause men everywhere to say that it has atrophied its will. But if the church will free itself from the shackles of a deadening status quo, and, recovering its great historic mission, will speak and act fearlessly and insistently in terms of justice and peace, it will enkindle the imagination of mankind and fire the souls of men, imbuing them with a flowing and ardent love for truth, justice, and peace. Men far and near will know the

---

2. 1 Tim. 2:4, rsv.

church as a great fellowship of love that provides light and bread for lonely travelers at midnight.[3]

In this century it is the role of the church to keep on fighting for justice and for righteousness and to be the leaven of society.

One way the church can seek to bring its moral power and its resources to bear in the struggle for justice is through the ministry of the pulpit. In this day it is the responsibility of the minister to keep on reminding America that the political crisis, the social crisis and the economic crisis are symptomatic of a far deeper moral crisis. The minister must keep reminding America that the bitter summers of discontent and rioting must be dealt with as evidence of a far more serious malady. The pulpit, as the focal point of the conscience of the nation, must keep on pointing to the causes of Watts and Newark and Detroit and Milwaukee until all America summons its resources for that radical social reform which will lessen the danger of further violence. While it is, obviously, the role of the pulpit to denounce the riots as destructive and disruptive, it is its role, too, to keep the alternatives in sharp focus. On the one hand, America can treat the symptoms as the disease by focusing on the riots with an increasingly repressive police tactic. Such an approach treats cancer with a band-aid while the real tumor continues its malignant spread. On the other hand, America can summon up her untapped reservoir of resources and provide low-income housing, employment for the hard-core unemployed, and quality education in the ghettos. Then America can move to challenge the racist soil that has nourished such discrimination.

The most ludicrous anomaly of the 1970s in the United States is related to the massive social reforms that are so desperately needed. No one who is familiar with the vast power of the federal government doubts that we have the resources to eradicate the ghettos of every city. And, yet, we lack the will to bring that reform to life and reality. Lyndon

---

3. Martin Luther King, Jr., *Strength To Love* (New York: Harper and Row, 1963), p. 47.

Baines Johnson rode the crest of optimism and confidence with which the people of the United States faced this decade into the White House. His State of the Union message of 1965 was directed toward social progress, and people everywhere were full of hope and optimism. The Civil Rights Bill of 1964, the poverty program with the Economic Opportunity Act as its heart, the model cities program, all were attempts to mobilize the strength, power and resources of the United States for a pitched battle against those social evils that plagued so many citizens. And, yet, we put a higher priority on the Vietnam struggle than we do on the struggle of the downtrodden and the deprived. It is the role of the pulpit to sound the alarm, to mobilize the resources available to the church, and to awaken the sleeping conscience of the nation to the plight of so many millions of citizens. The words of Amos hit us hard. He who claims to be a disciple of Jesus Christ in this generation cannot allow the plight of God's children to be passed by unnoticed.

III. Involvement with the Alienated

Up to this juncture I have highlighted the task of the church as concerned involvement and the task of the pulpit as a prophetic word dramatizing the nature of the human struggle as fundamentally moral. Now, what is the role of the individual Christian in the "war against poverty"? Is there a role the individual can fulfill beyond the task of the corporate church? How does one who is sensitive to human hurt identify with those who are poor, dispossessed, alienated and estranged?

Obviously, this is the level on which the real issue will be resolved. It is true that the federal government must mobilize our total resources to provide hope where despair is overwhelming and confidence where pessimism rules. But the individual must find a place to take hold before the debilitating effects of poverty are uprooted. The federal government can and must provide visible symbols of its concern in the form of jobs for the hard-core unemployed and housing for the low-income family. But it is up to individuals to get involved in the problem at the grass-roots level.

The question is, "How?" One way would be for a concerned family to become interested in an underprivileged family, to visit them, go into their home. Very often such homes are deprived of even the fundamental knowledge that we assume as part of our middle-class upbringing. The wife and mother can demonstrate how she functions as a home manager, as a parent, as a purchasing agent, as a guardian of health for her family, how she responds to the demands placed on her as a wife and mother. The husband and father must take the time to demonstrate how he functions in his own home. The privileged family must have a basic knowledge of the community resources that are available for the underprivileged so that response can be made immediately for any crisis, regardless of its dimension. I am not advocating transferring our middle-class values to someone else but rather being pragmatic.

This is a hazardous undertaking; it means making ourselves vulnerable to the contentions, bickerings, and feudings of another family. It means learning how to relate to other people as persons for whom Christ suffered redemptively. We must come to a new understanding of ourselves and our motives, and any paternalism with which we begin such an adventure must be confessed. We will have to learn how to relate meaningfully to families who are hostile or suspicious of our motives. Needy people are not always lovable; the high ideals with which we begin will wear thin, and we will need to be reinforced and strengthened for the continuing task.

At this point the church moves to center stage again. Assuming that the people of God who presently compose the Christian church in America are the persons who will be involved, the church must be the source of nourishment. As John Claypool observes, ". . . this is the challenge before us, and I do not think we have yet found the structure that will both create and sustain the saints of the twentieth century." He continued, in a sermon to his Crescent Hill congregation of Louisville, "I have grave doubts about many of our present ways of doing things, but no doubt at all that we must find some style of spiritual life and some shape of structure that holds the name of Jesus together with the giving of cups of cold water." The church must find a way of structuring itself so that it can be a source of support, encouragement and training for those who would attempt such a task. I see no other way of ever winning this "war against poverty." The church must be about the business of helping people understand themselves and those whom they serve. It must be a nourishment to those whose creative energies are sapped by the struggle of relating meaningfully and helpfully to the deprived.

Unless the church is redemptively involved in the world into which its faith constrains it, the church is a "religion without righteousness" and renders itself as fit for nothing except to be looked on with disdain. And so the living word of God comes to chasten and chide us in "Christian" America! He who would serve *God* is he who is serving the *disinherited* of the earth.

In his play *A Thousand Clowns*, Herb Gardner has a scene in which Arnold, the conformist who sold his soul for thirty thousand dollars a year, says of himself to his brother Murray, who hasn't sold out yet:

> I'm willing to deal with the available world, and I do not choose to shake it up, but to live with it. There's the people who spill things and the people who get spilled on. I do not choose to notice the stain, Murray.[4]

Arnold was expressing the view of many who claim the church yet deny their Lord. This has been the stance of many Christians and much of the church for long enough! It is the role of the people of God to soil and stain their hands in the service of a humanity whose creator is the Lord!

---

4. Herb Gardner, *A Thousand Clowns* (New York: Random House, 1962), p. 6.

3. HOSEA

An Everlasting Mercy

Scripture: Hosea 6:6, 11:4, 12:6, 14:4

Henry Ward Beecher was a nineteenth-century Hosea when he mounted his pulpit on September 19, 1860. At his side stood a girl who had been brought on consignment from her owner in Washington. Beecher was the minister of the famed Plymouth Church in Brooklyn. In a sense the girl was on the auction block there at the front of the church. The anti-slavery movement was at its crest. Beecher, with his sister Harriet Beecher Stowe who was the author of *Uncle Tom's Cabin*, was a leader in the movement to abolish slavery. And Beecher was challenging his congregation to give the $800 necessary to buy her from her owner. The congregation rose to the challenge and pledged the amount necessary to purchase her freedom.

Sixty-eight years later in 1928, Mrs. James Hunt appeared at the Plymouth Church one Sunday. She climbed nimbly up beside the pulpit and stood in the same spot where she had stood as a child-slave. In a quiet, cultured voice she told the story of that day when she had thought God was so far away and had suddenly heard his voice in the words of Henry Ward Beecher as he spoke to her, "My child, you are now free!"

There is a striking parallel between this incident and the

historical circumstances which surround the prophetic message of Hosea. Hosea's personal experience gave birth to the writings of the Old Testament which contain his name. Out of his own suffering, Hosea wrote of an everlasting mercy in the way God relates to his creatures. Hosea, too, went to the slave auction, bought a slave, and brought her back to the freedom of his home. But the similarity ends there. The slave girl who stood in the Plymouth Church had not abused her relationship to Beecher; she had not been married to him, and she was innocent of anything deserving the punishment of slavery. Hosea went to a slave auction and bought back the wife who had deserted him for her paramour.

Hosea had "an everlasting mercy" for his wife, and from the crucible of his own suffering love he caught a reflection of that divine love which is everlasting. John Masefield has given us a twentieth-century look at divine love in his poem *The Everlasting Mercy*, the story of Saul Kane and his fight against God. It is from that poem that I have taken the title for this chapter.

I. Legalism and Rejection

I begin with the contention that Hosea's problems started with his harsh, legalistic understanding of life. He was a preacher with but one theme—the sinfulness of man. He tolled only that bell which spoke of the judgment of God upon the sin of the people.

During this time he married a charming girl with a charmless name, Gomer. The first years of their marriage were happy. Hosea could have said of Gomer what one of Katherine Anne Porter's characters, Wilhelm Freytag, said of his wife in *Ship of Fools*, "Life goes on better whenever she is around." Theirs was a rich and meaningful relationship.

In this early stage of life Hosea decided to illustrate his preaching with his own experience. Had not God loved Israel? Had not God given his heart to Israel? Had not God joined himself in a covenant to his people? And Israel had refused to respond to that solicitude of God. The "austere restraints of a holy love" were rejected. Hosea could not hold back his wrath against a people who withdrew from their covenant relationship to God. His sermons of judgment became harsher and harsher. What began as love seemed now to be becoming unattractive.

Illustrative of the harsh, judgmental tone of his prophetic utterances upon the sin of the people was the bizarre way he had of naming his children. The names indicated his legalistic understanding of life, his insensitivity to human feelings and his perverted apprehension of the nature of God. His first child was named Jezreel. This was a Hebrew term associated with some of the bloodiest chapters in Israel's history. It was like naming a son Valley Forge, Alamo, Vicksburg, Iwo Jima, Saigon. Because the prophet Hosea was staunchly opposed to the jingoistic policies of the king, he made his son a visible portrayal of his opposition to militarism.

Indeed, Hosea used his family to demonstrate against the government. Thus, with his child as a picket sign, Hosea became the first anti-war demonstrator of antiquity. One of the most significant prophets of the Old Testament initiated protest on moral grounds. So the "peace movement" so prominently a part of the American political and social scene has its precedent in biblical religion as well as in history.

There is insight for us moderns here. Those who are so quick to condemn the Benjamin Spocks, the William Sloan Coffins, the Martin Luther Kings, the Cotesworth Pickney Lewises, and the Robert McAfee Browns should analyze this biblical precedent before they castigate anyone who has the courage to protest responsibly against the Vietnam conflict. I doubt that anyone could construe Hosea of aiding and abetting Egypt by his opposition. The condemnation of all protest as irresponsible has more than an aura of irresponsibility to it.

The modern parallel is such as to summon the sensitive conscience to outspoken protest. As *The Christian Century* put it so pungently, the protesters

> . . . do not wage chemical warfare 8,000 miles from home against men, women and children; they do not haughtily ignore the

reprimands the United States receives from almost every civilized people in the world; they do not recklessly and defiantly tweak the nose of the Chinese dragon, boasting that it is their purpose to contain China; they do not act as though it were their divine destiny to impose the will of the United States on more than a billion people in Asia; they do not wage on massive scale a war that neither the people of the United States nor their Congress authorized; they do not push the world closer to the final nuclear holocaust; they do not in their fury burn men's daily bread.[1]

Such protest may yet be the catalyst to awaken our national conscience. Then an aroused national conscience can force Congress to heed the deafening silence of ballots cast for more humane candidates. Protest may very well be the means whereby our foreign policy is purged of its stance as the "purveyor of violence."

When his second child was born, a daughter, Hosea named her "Unloved." She was a living illustration of Hosea's contention that God metes out stern judgment against a nation that had denied its covenant with God. The third child was named "Stranger." Hosea's assertion through her was that Israel's sin had made the nation a stranger to the providential purpose of God for his people. Israel had cut herself off from God, and therefore she was a fugitive, a vagabond, a stranger to God. So most of Hosea's message to this point is rooted in legalism and rejection and judgment.

II. God's Extravagant Mercy

This brings us to that segment of Hosea's experience in which God's everlasting mercy is revealed. The harmonious relationship between Hosea and Gomer had been deteriorating for some time. Hosea was so stern and harsh in his goodness that he made it easy for Gomer to justify and rationalize her return to her former philandering. And the gossip circulating about town was that the children born to Gomer were not Hosea's. So Gomer returned to the life of a prof-

---

1. "Thousands Rebuke the Pentagon," An Editorial, *The Christian Century*, November 1, 1967, p. 1390.

ligate and sought accepting love from a paramour. Hosea's life from this point on is radically altered.

The prophet reacts to all of this in a strange way. Most of us would have reacted with the strongest kind of hostility toward a woman who had openly betrayed our love and trust. The chances are that we would have lashed out with a righteous fury at her as the very epitome of irresponsibility and unrespectability. John Claypool expresses it this way: "Yet, as he faced this unbelievable affront and agony, the dominant feeling of his heart was not what we would normally expect. . . . What he felt more than anything else was unquenchable love for her. Instead of moving him to fiery indignation, her tragic plight aroused the springs of sorrow deep within him, and he knew beyond a shadow of doubt that what he really wanted was his wife won back and restored. And so we see this staggering love acted out, for Hosea went to the slave block where she was then imprisoned and put down fifteen pieces of silver and three and one-half sacks of barley for her ransom and then moved once more to woo and win back his beloved but faithless wife."

Hosea met the situation with humility and courage. After much soul-searching and after the rigorous spiritual exercise of self-examination, this domestic tragedy became a source of illumination on his own harsh goodness and on his understanding of the nature of God. The trauma of his own grief became the threshold whereby he discovered the deepest truth of God's self-disclosure. The very experience that leads some people away from God opened up new vistas of understanding for him. He was able to see himself more clearly, to become more sensitive to human travail in life and to understand God as one whose redemptive grace and forgiveness is wrought out through suffering.

Do you see why I have used the title of Masefield's poem to capture the essence of this prophetic message? "Everlasting mercy" is accurately descriptive of the reaction of Hosea to Gomer. Somewhere in the crucible of his own personal agony Hosea's emphasis had been radically modified. Whereas he had had a message of judgment on man's sin, now his emphasis shifted to the incredible, extravagant mercy of God.

This is the precise juncture at which the prophetic burden of Hosea becomes such a source of illumination. His emphasis is upon God's mercy, grace and suffering love and thereby his prophecy is a high-water mark of the Old Testament.[2] Norman H. Snaith defines that unrelenting love as "persistent, determined, unfailing covenant-love by which God showed His mercy to Israel . . . in spite of all their rebellion and waywardness."[3] It is a love which "nothing can destroy."[4]

His thought anticipates the New Testament teaching of the meaning of suffering, redemptive love. The amazing thing is that this truth gripped him within the sordid events of his own experience. Most of us expect profound insights to come from days when life is flourishing with prosperity, not from privation. But this usually doesn't happen. Luxury fattens the body, dulls the conscience, and makes the mind sluggish and inert. In reality, it takes the rigor of demanding days to summon forth from the depth strength enough to wrestle with the silent agonies of human existence.

Moreover, modern man feels that the issues of life are decided by power, that power shapes destiny and redeems the sordid circumstances of personal living. When Hosea affirms that redemption and wholeness come through suffering love, he is enunciating a truth that is foreign to the twentieth century. We affirm that the real deliverance from crippling fear, from the paralysis of despair, from the fragmentation of the common life, and from the ghettos of meaninglessness comes through power. But the shape of God's deliverance is ever the same—weakness, suffering, agony, a cross.

The agony of Hosea's love was a window through which he caught a fresh glimpse of the suffering love God has

---

2. H. W. Robinson calls Hosea's theology one of the two "deepest moral conceptions of God which the Old Testament contains." See his *The Religious Ideas of the Old Testament* (London: Duckworth, 1952), p. 69.

3. Norman H. Snaith, *The Distinctive Ideas of the Old Testament* (London: Epworth, 1953), p. 173.

4. *Ibid.*, p. 113.

always offered to his people. Hosea came to recognize that genuine love is more than the austere restraints of a legal code. It is a love which in its free-flowing openness to someone can be refused and rejected. It is a love which refuses to abandon its self-imposed exile from the one to whom the love is extended until the loved responds to the lover. Withdrawn in exile such love awaits the time when the sulking disobedience and refusal will end. Love withholds the impulse to batter down the barriers. This is the agony and suffering of love.

The suffering comes as a result of a commitment to the value of a person who has been created free. He is free to respond in love and he is free to refuse. Such love is in a continuous struggle to contain itself. Love cares but refuses to enter into a man's need until he throws his life open to love. Suffering love allows the loved one to be free to rebel, to sin and, thereby, to mature. As Paul Scherer puts it so splendidly, authentic love "stands there with its hands gripped tightly behind its back, biting its lips." That is love suffering and caring. It is a heroic love, for it accepts rejection and waits in solitude for the loved one to return.

This, then, is the reason the message of Hosea is a forerunner of the New Testament. It speaks of that quality of mercy and unfailing love so exemplified in Jesus. It characterizes God as one whose love comes through the pangs of suffering. He causes God to cry out, as he had done in the swirling emptiness of his own loss, "I taught Ephraim how to walk, holding him in my arms! How can I give him up! How can I let him go?" This is the same understanding of God which is found in the parables of the lost sheep, the lost coin and the two lost sons.

III. God's Everlasting Mercy

What, then, is the conclusion of it all? In Hosea's writings you are seeing the bared heart of God. His is "an everlasting mercy" that never gives up on a man. His pierced hand is forever knocking. The searching scrutiny of his gaze haunts Everyman. His pursuit is unrelenting.

Yet, to what extent can we accept and participate in the experience of this prophet Hosea? Can we crash through our natural tendency to refuse to love people? Can we overcome our instincts to be hard, immovable, and unforgiving? Can we put over into human relationships an everlasting mercy? Can we who have been forgiven learn to be forgiving? There is something inordinately "wrong if we can accept everlasting mercy for ourselves and yet show no hope or compassion for others. There is a real link between divine mercy and human mercy. If I am saved by the astonishing grace of God, what could be more logical than that I should love my enemies? . . . If God's mercy is big enough to see worth in me when I am evil and to accept me back and even work to initiate this, then such an attitude towards others ought to characterize my life in Him." [5]

As long as Hosea laid emphasis upon justice and judgment for sinners and on sin he was a stranger to mercy. But when he came to understand that God loves us not primarily because we are lovable but because he is loving, then the prophet became more concerned with mercy than with judgment. This is precisely the direction many moderns must take. They are conscious of man's sin and lawlessness, and therefore are concerned with judgment, punitive measures against the lawbreaker, and with legal action. But when we learn from the crucible of our own experience that there is love in the heart of things, then concern is for redemption, forgiveness and mercy.

My plea is for the healing and creative power of everlasting mercy. Such mercy sees people as persons, uniquely and infinitely meaningful. It sees God as the Creator who made man in his image. It sees a self-willed, sinful, self-asserting, rebellious creation that has rejected the eternal love and everlasting mercy of the Creator. But more than this, it sees the divine dimension that is present in every person and keeps on loving until every human life is open to that love.

---

5. From a sermon by John Claypool. Used with his permission.

Francis Thompson writes of man's flight and God's everlasting pursuit in these beautiful words:

> I fled Him, down the nights and down the days;
> I fled Him, down the arches of the years;
> I fled Him, down the labyrinthine ways
> Of my own mind; and in the mist of tears
> I hid from Him, and under running laughter.
> Up vistaed hopes I sped;
> And shot, precipitated,
> Adown Titanic glooms of chasmèd fears,
> From those strong Feet that followed, followed after.
> But with unhurrying chase,
> And unperturbèd pace,
> Deliberate speed, majestic instancy,
> They beat—and a Voice beat
> More instant than the Feet—
> "All things betray thee, who betrayest Me." [6]

No one has ever been able to escape the mercy and love of
God because God pursues us eternally and hopefully.

And we to whom such mercy has been proffered can best
express our gratitude by being merciful to all God's fugitive
sons and daughters. Then their flight can end and every fugitive from God's mercy can find fulfillment. All of this world's
Gomers can know that the nourishing graciousness of a God
of mercy still has a place for them.

---

6. Francis Thompson, "The Hound of Heaven."

4. ISAIAH OF JERUSALEM
When God Is Real

Scripture: Isaiah 1:21, 28:16–17, 37:35

As many times as I had read the story of the experience of
Isaiah of Jerusalem in the Temple in the year King Uzziah
died, the depth of the trauma into which Isaiah had been
plummeted had never dawned on me until one tragic day in
November of 1963. Until then I had not been totally conscious of the devastation wrought by such a loss. But that
day the whole nation was plunged into grief and despair
over the assassination of John Fitzgerald Kennedy. The
numbing shock and overwhelming sorrow closed in on me
and bolted my mind against any new vistas of understanding.
As the day wore on I turned to the sixth chapter of Isaiah and
immediately that which had eluded me now gripped me. It is
the testimony of the centuries that God, somehow and some-
way, breaks into our lives at the precise moment of our
deep need. Often, God becomes real at the exact point of our
direst despair. I found it true that God became more real at a
time when life seemed empty, sterile, and devoid of meaning.

Isaiah's travail of soul came from the death of King
Uzziah. Grief drove him to the Temple to mourn his loss. He
had known no other ruler and Uzziah's death was a tragedy
of major proportions. This was the end of an era. It was as if
God had turned away from him and deserted him, that

meaninglessness, heartache, and misery were his unending destiny.

The words, "In the year that King Uzziah died I saw the Lord," mark the birthday of a prophetic soul and the beginning of a new quality in his spiritual pilgrimage. The restless questionings which crowded in upon Isaiah clamored for some kind of an answer. And it was in the tremendous mystery of God's presence that the answer came as the young prophet saw himself and the people of Judah in a new light.

How did it happen that Isaiah saw God and how did this vision take him back into his generation? God's presence disciplined his restless spirit and called him back to his prophetic task. The deepening sense of God's presence in the Temple quickened his imagination, made sensitive his questing spirit, influenced his inquisitive mind, haunted his commitment to serve, and colored his theological understanding. Scholars have suggested that it might have been New Year's day, when, in a symbolic ceremony, it is thought, God was represented as coming to the Temple to chasten the people for their waywardness and to announce their destiny for the days ahead. This was the high drama of that day of worship when Isaiah entered the Temple.

Isaiah lived in one of the most difficult eras of Hebrew history. Assyria was the dominant world power and she was beginning to assert herself. Judah was caught in the dilemma of her desire for independence and self-determination on the one hand, and the need for a security enhanced by an alliance with Assyria on the other. But the Kingdom of Judah had lost its monarch. The nation which had fared so well under the guidance, impetus and benevolence of Uzziah's reign was now in eclipse. Powerful Assyria was threatening to advance. Tiglath-pileser III was even then contemplating extending his invasion of northern Israel all the way south to Judah. So, Isaiah, hoping against hope, was ready to hear a healing word from God. But what startled him was that there was no word of God for Judah; *he* was the word. Who shall bear the burden of the Lord to Judah? Who shall go?

The question came with power to the sensitive aristocrat, and he agreed to embody in himself and his prophetic message the live and lively word of God for Judah. Isaiah 6 represents a simple and clear demand that he *be* the word of God for Judah.

The writings of Isaiah of Jerusalem are preserved in chapters 1 through 39 and they bear the authentic stamp of an aristocrat. He began his prophetic ministry in the year of King Uzziah's death, 740 B.C., and continued his work through the reigns of Jotham, Ahaz, and Hezekiah. He was of royal lineage, educated and urbane, steeped in the religious training of his day, a confidant of kings. However, his background, training and family heritage seemed to dispose him to an antipathy toward change in the structures of society. In reality, Isaiah of Jerusalem was a part of the power structure or, to say the least, obligated to it. He was a member of an aristocratic family that was part of the Establishment. As Paterson puts it succinctly, he was possessed of an "aristocratic horror of any upheaval in the existing order of society. . . . Isaiah was a born aristocrat and could visualize no society without aristocrats in the seats of the mighty." [1]

If this is the case then where are there to be found social implications in the oracles of Isaiah of Jerusalem? We need to remember that every man is a child of his own historical framework. The insights of the greatest prophets are broken, fragmentary, and partial. Even with the brilliant insights that are found in their writings the ultimate disclosure of God awaits Jesus Christ. The insight of one generation waits for the succeeding generation to plumb its depth. Even though Isaiah would have been suspicious of any radical upheaval in the social structure, he was inflamed by the graft of public officials, the shallow vanity of the idle rich, and the insatiable greed of many. Thus, we cannot say that Isaiah had no concern for justice except as it is mediated through present structures.

---

1. John Paterson, *The Goodly Fellowship of the Prophets* (New York: Scribner's, 1950), p. 73.

Although Isaiah does not preach drastic social change he does speak of the very spring which nourishes that change so desperately necessary in our generation. Because he was a part of the Establishment is not a sufficient reason to claim that he was insensitive to the poor and needy. The important thing to remember about Isaiah is that God became overwhelmingly real to him in the experience in the Temple. And when God becomes real, then changes begin to occur.

I. Celebrating Life

When God becomes refreshingly real we are open to a mood of celebrating life. A vital understanding of God often diverts life into new channels. A fresh perception of the divine can sharpen one's sensitivity to the joys of the creation. Man's pattern of existence needs an exhilarating affirmation of the joys of life to keep it wholesome. Man needs to learn to celebrate life with a reckless abandon.

Somewhere in recent history the Christian church in America has succumbed to the numbing effects of a rigid Calvinism, and life has been robbed of its mood of adventure, color, and romance. A virgin nation needed the structure of a Puritanical attitude toward pleasure. The rugged existence of America's western frontiers was difficult at best. So, building on the cleavage of a Calvinistic determinism concerning man's ultimate destiny, the frontiersman learned a respect for the rigor of a toil that would and could wrest a home from the wilderness. He accepted as a necessity the morbid pessimism that divested life of its celebrative qualities. Sacrifice, effort, drudgery, and the concomitant extraordinarily high premium on work were the guidelines of his existence.

Although the structure which made such a view essential to survival no longer exists, modern man had not been able to shuck his outmoded understanding of the innate and primary value of work. This commitment to work as the *only* cardinal virtue is critical of a mood of celebrating life as futile and wasteful. Now, with the automation and cybernation of much of industry, work has a lesser value to our culture. It must be understood as an activity whose value is related to providing the means for qualitative existence.

Another factor involved in this debilitating attitude we have toward life is the fact that it is easy to get values out of balance. Dr. E. J. Kepler of the Mayo Clinic concluded from his work as a physician that we "devote a preponderance of our time and energy to the fulfilment of only a fraction of ourselves." It is not that we view the mood of celebrating life as evil; it is just that in our quest for things and security and status and power we emphasize the *means* of living rather than the *end* of living. This is the pervading sin of modern America. The result is that in our pursuit for the status symbols of an affluent society we lose sight of life itself and there is little time left to joyously affirm and celebrate life.

How does one discover and recover the mood of joyous celebration? How does one learn to live life with exhilaration and passion? He must return to those springs from which his life is nourished and sustained. He must relearn the fact that he is a creature whose significance has been given by the Creator. He must, as Isaiah, enter his Temple wherein God's graciousness can break into his life with a creative affirmation of his worth. In biblical categories this happens when he discovers his sin as a denial of his finitude, and when he throws life open to God's redemptive love in faith and commitment. Thus that capacity to relate lovingly to the Creator is renewed.

Only then does life fall into place. As the gifted minister Dr. Melvin E. Wheatley of Los Angeles, California, puts it, "our bodies become trustees of his energies; our minds become media for his truths; our families become cameos of his kingdom; our social concerns of justice and mercy become instruments of his will and his peace." This is exactly what happened when God became vitally real to Isaiah in the Temple. Life fell into place and he was prepared to enter the everyday world with a passion and a conviction to serve God.

The faith that has lost this capacity to celebrate, to venture, to dare is not the religion of Jesus. It has lost that source of

strength which enabled Isaiah to respond, "Here am I; send
me." The faith which alienated Jesus from the prosaic religious leaders of his day was one that gallantly flung life into
the clash between the kingdom of this world and the kingdom of God. It was a way of life with a contagious, infectious
mood of celebrating.

This is the quality Isaiah gained as God became refreshingly real to him, that nourished his soul and steeled him for
an abandonment to the service of God. It was a quality of
spirit and a sensitivity of soul that enabled him to bear the
burden of God to his people Judah.

Without this mood pervading his writings Isaiah's message
would be sterile and barren indeed. With it his living word is
resurrected to life in every generation which needs fresh
courage to serve God including ours. Today we have a frenzy
of countless radical revolutions. A fresh apprehension of God
with all his stringent moral demands is the only aspect of
religion that can enable a man to stand his ground amid
these revolutions, to enter into life with an abandon, a daring, a
mood of celebration which asserts that God shall yet claim this
creation for his eternal purpose. So the vision of Isaiah of
Jerusalem is a call to modern man to live each day to its fullest,
celebrating life as a gift of God. Then he is prepared to come to
grips with his vital role in which life involves him as a servant
of God.

II. A Creative, Redeemed Minority

Secondly, Isaiah contends that whatever justice is attained
in society will come through a humanity renewed and redeemed. In the brightness of his vision of God, Isaiah saw
himself as he really was. Following his confession of his
unworthiness and his commitment to God, his insight set a
dream into his mind. His great view of God moved him to
dream of a new creation and a new humanity. He caught
a glimpse of a new dimension to human life, and he came
to believe that the new humanity was the key to justice and
mercy among men.

Isaiah saw the drunken debauchery, the avarice and greed,

the rebellious self-asserting of the rich; he saw the predicament of the poor. He saw the hollow and perfunctory religious rituals, the abuses of the festivals and the unthinking, habitual quality of religious life. Being an aristocrat who believed that the only live option was in the hands of a renewed kingdom after the order of David (see Isa. 9, 11), he despaired of the conversion of the masses from their evil. Yet, he was convinced that a creative minority would respond to God when he became refreshingly real. This new humanity was to be a remnant, a new order of creation.

In our day, if ever justice becomes more than an illusive shadow for much of American society there must come a new order of humanity. And this is happening as God moves history toward his new creation. God is at work in "the secular city" in unexpected places. As Dr. Jitsuo Morikawa, Secretary of the Division of Evangelism of the American Baptist Home Mission Societies, said to the Riverside Church in New York, "God's mysterious but glorious activity of reconstituting the world occurs in unpredictable and unexpected secular events." So God is at work in history "liberating men from the slavery of being merely used, humanizing the world toward the new society, freeing man to be authentically human, breaking walls of separation."

It is the role of the church to testify to and bear witness of that emerging new humanity which is symbolized by Christ's life, death, and resurrection. It is a new dimension of community wherein the self dies that newly created and resurrected life may be fulfilled. To be the church, then, is to be vulnerable to death. The church must demonstrate in its corporate life that the brokenness and fragmentation of human life can be healed as the creative force of God is turned loose into life through the death of self.

The church is to become a symbol of hope, a colony of the new humanity. The church must seek, therefore, to identify with the dispossessed, the disinherited of the world. Where human dignity is denied, where social structures segregate and divide, where the inhumanity of man to man is obvious —here the church has a clear call to be involved. To do less is to deny mission on the ragged edges of history.

In his sermon to the Riverside congregation, Dr. Morikawa maintained that there are tiny colonies which are the first-fruits of a new humanity all over the world. He defined these clandestine movements as the activity of God in the dramatic events of the secular world; for example, he dared to ask if God is working in the disturbing ways of Black Power. So, if the church is to remain a viable symbol of the new humanity, he contended that it must identify with these clandestine colonies of a new humanity.

> If the church is called to the dangerous vocation of living at the vanguard of history, where the future is breaking in and the old is passing away at the point of history's crises, then the church is called to costly identification and participation in these tiny colonies of rebirth and resurrection, to bring them into historical visibility. The church is called to witness, to a *public* witness and disclosure of these unpopular events and movements which subvert the old obsolete structures of tyranny and ignorance and bring into being a new social arrangement. And *this* is the church's place in evangelism, giving public witness by word and participation to the events of God's newness erupting into history, living always on the boundary between the present and future, being a people of the future, living the future already in the present, and bearing the cross of suffering implicit in rebirth and resurrection toward the New Creation.[2]

There is no other way to justice in our time than through a humanity renewed and redeemed. This was Isaiah's contention and he gave objective reality to his assertion when he named his firstborn son "a remnant shall return."

III. Concern for the Cities

There is another gem in the writings of Isaiah of Jerusalem—his concern for the cities, chiefly Jerusalem. He noted that the "faithful city" had prostituted justice (1:21), but he was convinced that God would renew her, make her a bulwark against the enemy (26:1–21), and make her the struc-

---

2. From Dr. Jitsuo Morikawa's sermon "Toward the New Creation" and used with his permission.

tural cornerstone for a new order of society (28:16). In fact, God would preserve the city as the arena in which the holy remnant would serve God (37:35) for his own sake and for King David's sake.

Because the aristocratic prophet was reared in Jerusalem he was naturally concerned with the survival of the city. Jerusalem surrounded him with all the pungent odors of a teeming humanity and the discordant music of a thousand daily concerns. Its pulsating, vibrant vitality was always clamoring for his attention even in the midst of a tense era of Hebrew history. Moreover, its misery, its poverty and its dehumanizing touch confronted his sensitive conscience and made him painfully aware of its desperate need of God's mercy. All of this, then, is reason enough to anticipate a prophet concerned for the welfare of the city.

I can understand, for the city has always held an attraction for me. Its masses of humanity beckon to me. Its skyscrapers slashing the horizon mesmerize me with their daily rebuffs of the erosion of nature. But, of course, I have never had to experience the utter frustration of trying to convince a landlord that he must bring the house up to city codes. I have never had to walk the tightrope between the street gangs and their switchblades. I have never tried to escape the ghetto only to meet the onslaught of the threats of potential neighbors. I have never had to face the hostility of a people whose prejudiced efforts were triggered by the mere fact of my color. I have never had to adjust to the subculture of a poverty which emasculates me of my dignity. I have never had to seek education in a substandard schoolroom which threatened my potential as a productive member of society. I have never had to face the unexpected and unanticipated loss of the only means of survival due to automation. So, like so much of affluent America, I have never been prepared by experience to understand the crisis of the city, as Ertha Kitt dared to point out to her host, Mrs. Lyndon B. Johnson.

The point that I am seeking to make is so obvious that it is trite. The major issue of the United States on the domestic front is the crisis of the city. No one doubts this. And there are many reasons that make this the case. The sociological factors that have contributed to this crisis are varied. The hurly-burly of city life clothes neighbors in an anonymity that breaks the communion of man to man into a thousand fragments. The depersonalization of an industrial economy with its IBM cards, social security numbers, and zip codes has frozen the concern of the human spirit. The nomadic nature of 25 percent of the population tempts many to excuse themselves from any personal responsibility and involvement in the common life. In short, there has been an almost total loss of a sense of community in the city, and without it, millions of people are ignored.

The situation created by these sociological factors is complicated by the tragic history of Negro slavery and its companion and colleague, segregation. This historical factor has contributed to the discrimination of unequal employment opportunity for minority groups, closed housing, and poor educational advantages. Here, then, are the real roots of the mob violence, looting, arson, murder and rioting. The injustice of this kind of a social structure has perpetuated an intolerable burden on a large segment of our society.

What is the church to do? God summons the church to lay itself open to the pain and agony of the city in crisis, to risk our institutional strength in the warfare to be waged. He calls us to be willing to suffer with the people of the city. As Robert Raines puts it, God calls the church to be "an oasis of mercy in a desert of dehumanization." He calls us to keep on asserting that the crisis of the cities is fundamentally a moral crisis. He calls us to become involved in eliminating the inequities of our social structure. He summons us to an involvement in the issues of peace, race, poverty, open housing, and unity; God calls us to incarnate the spirit of Jesus Christ in the corporate life of the nation. The church must bring its moral power and its voice to the support of programs calling for jobs for unemployed and underemployed, open housing, expansion of all public services and facilities, quality education in slum areas, and other long-term or immediate proposals.

But there is still another word. Our involvement in social action must never degenerate into a bland humanism. The secularized dimension of our involvement must not become a substitute for the religious roots which gave birth to our sensitive concern for the crisis of the cities. There is the danger that our activism will become an escape whereby we refuse to face the chastening and disciplining word of God which is our ultimate nourishment. It is easy to seek to elude God in the city. The asphalt jungle offers multitudes of caverns in which to hide. But this is a perversion of Christianity, as Browne Barr suggests, "a religion without ecstasy." Our concern for the crisis of the city must be a "rapture not shorn of moral imperative but rather born of it and interlaced with it." [3]

The church must enter into the agony of the city. It must wrestle with hate, hostility, racism, poverty, closed housing, and slum ghettos until they yield justice. It must love with a love that holds nothing back, for the strength of love is its undefeatable quality. H. H. Farmer interprets this strength like this:

> . . . the only qualification for victory required of love is that it should be able to endure its most shattering defeat and yet still remain love. If it does that, it has still got the whip hand; for in its very weakness of defeat it has within it the invincible strength of remaining itself, and it will yet win its victory. As someone has said, "you cannot defeat defeat." Let man take every advantage of the seeming weakness of love, let them bruise and batter and seek utterly to smash it, as they did at the Cross; but let it still remain love, and in the end they will have to give up, and look upon what their hands have done, and break down in its presence. At some time or other the very weakness of love will cut them to the center of their being with more power than a two-edged sword. [4]

The truth is clear. A cross stood, centuries past, on the brow

3. Browne Barr, "Beyond Activism," *The Christian Century*, February 7, 1968, pp. 160–64.
4. H. H. Farmer, *Things Not Seen* (London: James Nisbet, Ltd., 1927), p. 143.

of a wind-swept and barren hill. All the hate of a city swept up the hill and nailed Love's son to the cross. But the cry comes back that the final judge is a history controlled by God.

That same hostility is sweeping its course across the nation and erecting its crosses in the cities. History's judgment is still to be rendered. And the verdict can only be swayed by the church as it scorns its institutional life in order to be resurrected triumphantly and joyfully, shepherding the new humanity of man's cities past the strongholds of our rebellion into the eternal city of God's grace and mercy. When God becomes real, then you, like Isaiah, will find that there is no live word from God unless *you are that word of God for America!*

Let us not despair of the cities. Let us return to those springs of creative energy from whose depths our nourishment comes. And, while there, let us soak our minds and consciences in the reality of God. Then, let us throw ourselves open to a mood of celebrating life, let us learn to live passionately as the church, God's twentieth-century remnant of hope, testifying to that emerging dimension of a new humanity. As the church flings itself into the agony of the cities to be crucified and resurrected to a new quality of service, the whole creation can be renewed and redeemed. Then the cities of men will become the cities of God as they are permeated with a new people of God!

5. MICAH

The Demanding Claim of Religion

Scripture: Micah 6:8, 7:18–19

The Christian gospel has two aspects: the proclamation of what God has done for us in Jesus Christ, and the affirmation of what is demanded of the disciple. And keeping both properly in balance is one of the difficult tasks of the preacher. It is all too easy to emphasize one to the the exclusion of the other. On the one hand, it is so easy to exult in the magnificence and beneficence of God's activity in Jesus Christ, to get caught up in the dramatic revelation of his redemptive mercy and loving graciousness and, thereby, to neglect the side of the gospel which I am calling "the demanding claim of religion." On the other hand, it is easy to lay so much emphasis on what God expects of a disciple that we lose sight of God's majestic goodness and sovereignty. The Reformation was a reaction against this kind of emphasis—religion had become a legalistic system in which one's meritorious performance of his duty earned his rightful access to the divine presence.

The Bible is full of the affirmation of what God has done for us. "God was in Christ reconciling the world unto himself," Paul tells us. John's Gospel affirms that "God so loved the world that he gave his only Son that whoever believes in him should not perish but have eternal life." God loved us before we could love him, and he did something for us before we could do anything for him. This is the very heart of the gospel. This is the lifting impetus that propelled the early church out into society to announce the fact of God's participation in life.

But there is another side to this matter, which is my concern in this chapter. It is the concern of the prophet Micah. Micah spoke of the demanding claim which religion lays on a man. His burden was that the children of Israel recognize that God demands a people who "do justly and love mercy and walk humbly" with him.

The facts about the prophet Micah are so few that to introduce him to you graphically is impossible. Of necessity the person of the prophet will have to remain somewhat obscure, even while his message stands out in bold relief. Micah was an unadorned and unsophisticated rustic whose ministry began in a small village some twenty-five miles from Jerusalem. He had the sturdy and rugged independence of a man who lives close to people and the land. He was a totally different personality from his contemporary Isaiah who was a confidant of royalty and an aristocrat. Micah was an earthy man, a small-town artisan. He possessed a deep-seated identification with and sympathy for the poor and despised. And his sermons were delivered, for the most part, on trips to Jerusalem.

I. Justice for the Poor

The heart of Micah's message is found in Micah 6:8: "What does the Lord require from you but to be just, to love mercy and to walk humbly with your God?" [1] The message of Micah is rooted in a fundamental concern for justice. Micah is preeminently the spokesman for the poor and the dispossessed. He represents "the forgotten man" and speaks for the inarticulate masses. His accent is the accent of the plain, blunt and direct spokesman. He speaks simply and

---

1. J. B. Phillips, *Four Prophets* (New York: The Macmillan Co., 1963), p. 156.

sincerely of the fact that the "demanding claim of religion" is for justice.

And what did he mean by justice? This noble and high-sounding word does not lend itself easily to a simple and clear-cut definition. Micah never stopped to define justice with logic and precision. And this is the case in modern life. We assume justice. If we are part of the Establishment then justice becomes an appeal for law and order, a cry for the rioting and pillaging to come to an end. If we are part of the disestablishment then justice becomes a basic concern for freedom and human rights. Speaking for the downtrodden the prophet Micah calls for a basic recognition of every man's rights. He calls for fair dealings between men. He calls for a solicitude for the oppressed, the exploited and the economically deprived. Parenthetically, it is interesting to note how much he sounds like a modern prophet standing in the asphalt jungles of our city ghettos calling for the fundamental rights of those who have been defrauded.

Micah, then, is a passionate advocate for justice. And he preaches justice because of two elementary presuppositions. The first is what he believes about God. In his own mind he is making an appeal to the only real standard there is for justice. It is not a standard that has evolved in the course of history as mores and conventions. It is a standard that is rooted in the very nature of God. In God all justice is rooted and grounded and issues forth from him as revelation to man. God deals fairly with men and they are to deal fairly with one another.

Micah is a passionate advocate of justice, also, because of what he believes about man. He believes that every man has native, inherent rights. Because he was created in the image of God, man has an inviolable dignity as a person. His personhood has some claim on justice. We all have equal rights and we ought to be treated with justice because we are all the children of one Father. Therefore, for Micah, the creation of man in the image of God is the fundamental basis for justice and the source of the demand for it.

Yes, we are to deal justly with one another; but God does

not deal with us solely on the basis of justice. He deals with us on the basis of his gracious concern and redeeming compassion. And this teaching is part of Micah's message.

II. The Creative Strength of Mercy

Micah writes of the creative strength of mercy. For the prophet Micah such a demand involves an understanding of the incredible mercy and kindness of God. God is incredible in his mercy, extravagant in his kindness, and everlasting in his love. Suppose that you had created this world and peopled it with creatures made in your own image. Suppose, also, that you had granted them perfect freedom and had written into their hearts a restless longing. Then, the next thing, these creatures were fighting and struggling to get on top. I wonder what you would do.

I can tell you what God did. He went down to live among those rebellious and self-seeking creatures to share their life with agonies and struggles. So, tabernacled in human flesh, God began his rendezvous with man. He demonstrated the fact of his compassionate, understanding grace. T. E. Lawrence of Arabia says that the Arabs taught him that "no man could be their leader except he ate their own food, wore their clothes, lived level with them and, yet, appeared better in himself." This is what God did. He knows our every temptation, our every burden, and our every weakness because of his rendezvous in the world. He knows and understands our common human lot. And the more the poor, wounded, guilty and straying fugitives of this world know of God's rendezvous in human life, the more they know that God cares with an extravagant mercy.

Still, as the gifted preacher Edmund A. Steimle writes,[2] God did more. And this quality of mercy is the most durable power in the world. This creative force, so beautifully exemplified in the life of Jesus Christ, is the most potent instrument available in mankind's quest for adventuresome life.

---

2. Edmund Steimle, "The Extravagant Kindness," *Are You Looking For God?* (Philadelphia: Fortress Press, 1957), pp. 146–54.

The "demanding claim of religion" and of the prophet Micah is for a life that lives out this creative quality of mercy. We must move out to keep our rendezvous with the world, treating every person with love and compassion. This kind of mercy is like God.

III. A Reverence of Spirit

Moreover, Micah delineates the "demanding claim of religion" as walking humbly with God. This means a renunciation of all human arrogance and selfishness so that one's life may be open to the invasion of God's gracious mercy. It is a reverence of spirit that seeks to be in tune with the Infinite. When the prophet speaks of "doing justly" he is referring to that integrity of character whereby one seeks to treat every man as his brother. When he speaks of "loving mercy" he is referring to that sympathy of heart and compassion of soul that wills the good of others. And when he comes to speak of "walking humbly with God" he is speaking of that reverence of spirit and humility of mind that opens life up to the identification of life with the divine life.

Now listen to a modern paraphrase [3] of the thrust of Micah's writing. He writes that God lays a rigorous claim on life.

You know well enough, you Christians, what is good! For what does the Lord require from you? Listen!
He requires justice from every man,
    But the courts provide injustice to the poor and freedom to the Hoffas—
        The church loves the rich who swell her coffers and only tolerates the poor—
        The factories rob the dignity of the working man—
            The hospitals charge for services not rendered
            and keep the well in beds that otherwise would be empty!
The Lord requires that all of you be just.
He requires mercy from man to man,
    For justice goes part of the way and mercy finishes the trek—

---

3. Paraphrase by the author.

Mercy to those in whom hurts and wounds abound—
Mercy heaped up and running over—
Mercy from one and all to one and all.
The Lord requires that all of you be merciful.
He requires humility in every man.
Humility in those whose pride denies their sinfulness—
Humility in those whose sinfulness is their source of pride—
Humility in those whose sinfulness goes unrecognized—
Humility in those whose humility is their pride.
The Lord requires that all of you be humble.

I can best summarize the message of Micah with an illustration suggested by Theodore P. Ferris. Suppose that you met a person on the New Jersey side of the Hudson River near New York City who was obviously a stranger and who didn't know where he was. Suppose, also, that he wanted to go to New York City but that he was not sure of the direction. At the moment he was walking toward Newark, in the opposite direction. You would tell him to turn around. "Do you see that building looming up over the horizon? That's the Empire State Building. That's the constant element. That's fixed. Walk in that direction and you will finally get to New York City."

Micah said that there is an unchanging element in the "demanding claim of religion," namely, that man shall do justly, love mercy and walk humbly with God. And only as one measures up to this constant demand can he claim to be a child of the Eternal.

6. ZEPHANIAH

Dark Is the Night

Scripture: Zephaniah 1:12–2:3

Homer's *Odyssey* is an epic poem which describes the wanderings of Ulysses after the siege of Troy. His trek took him on many fateful adventures. At one point in his journeyings it was his lot to sail between two perils. The only safety lay in steering an undeviating mid-course between the two. On the one hand was the dreadful monster Scylla. She had six heads and lived in a cavern on the face of a high cliff overlooking a narrow channel. From every ship that passed by she tried to seize a sailor in each mouth. On the opposite side of the narrow channel grew a wild fig tree and beneath it lay the hideous Charybdis who sucked in and regorged the sea. It was the hazardous fate of Ulysses to sail between these dual perils, seeking to avoid the loss of his crew to the monster and the loss of his ship to the whirlpool created by Charybdis. A course that was totally undeviating was absolutely necessary for survival.

There was a prophet of Israel to whom was given the task of plotting a course as straight as that required of Ulysses, and calling Israel to follow it. When we delve into the book bearing his name we are confronted with an undeviating message.

It is generally agreed that Zephaniah's prophetic ministry

67

ended previous to the reforms instituted by King Josiah and the discovery of the Deuteronomic scrolls. Therefore, the date 625 B.C. is almost universally accepted by the scholars. It is very probable that his ministry was an influential factor in the reforms inaugurated by King Josiah in 621 B.C. The burden of the prophet's message is threefold: He indicts his own people Israel, denounces the foreign hordes and nations, and envisions the future glory of Israel as a chastened and humbled minority. What is Zephaniah's message to our day? Is there a live word here for the people of God in this vigorous onslaught of Zephaniah against Israel?

I. A Message of Judgment

There is only one place to begin when you seek to wrestle with the meaning of Zephaniah for our day—with judgment. This is the major theme which Zephaniah pursues with an unrelenting tenacity. He sees a people, a nation and a world that have so totally alienated themselves from God that there is little hope. Israel, particularly, has so completely removed herself from the arena of life as God's redeemed and redeeming people that there is little recourse but their utter extermination.

The historical situation which warranted such condemnation of Israel is fairly clear. Zephaniah knew that Scythian hordes were poised on the borders threatening at any moment to strike with marauding bands. The invasion was imminent and Zephaniah viewed it as irrevocable. The idolatry of the people was so nearly complete that God would not turn back the Scythian invaders until they had served as the instrument of his judgment. If by some unknown and miraculous reversal of history they were to be stayed, then some other power in the dark, rumbling North would fell Israel with one fatal swoop.

The faithlessness of God's people was flagrantly obvious. The court of the king was a colorful tapestry of foreign fashions, idolatry was rank in public life, the prophets were eating at the king's table, buying his doctrine of expediency and security, so that prophetic utterances had degenerated to squeaking shadows of reality. The prophets gave the people what they wanted to hear in order that their sinfulness not be challenged—the kind of preaching that merely produces a continuing lack of sensitivity to human need. Surely, God would not tolerate such open disregard by his people.

Because of his understanding of sin and of God, Zephaniah promised judgment to come. He saw sin in all of its raw and harsh reality as selfish, prideful, idolatrous, rebellious, and disastrous. His understanding of sin as that self-imposed barrier between the individual and God, as the crushing pride of life, as inordinate self-concern was so overwhelming and so overpowering that he could not see how the hand of God's judgment could be stayed. He was so sensitive to the suffering and agony of sin he saw all about him that he couldn't hold back his prophetic denunciation. On the other side, he had such a high view of the divine sovereignty that he could see no ray of hope and viewed judgment as inevitable.

II. The Divine Control of Nature and History

Zephaniah sees God as controlling both nature and history and moving all things toward himself. God is not bound up with Israel and thereby set over against a hostile world. Rather, he is God of the whole world which is in rebellion against him. He is concerned not only with Israel but with the whole created universe. Hence, Zephaniah begins to crack the shell of isolationism and sectarianism and provincialism that has characterized Israel through so much of her history. Because of his perceptive understanding of God and of sin, Zephaniah begins to open up the eyes of his people to the universality of God.

There is as much for us to learn as there was for Zephaniah and Israel. I am afraid that we are a nation of provincials when it comes to our understanding of God. We are afraid to pursue the teaching that God is Lord for and of all the created universe. He is the Lord God of the Russians, the Red Chinese, and the Viet Cong just as surely as he is our God here in America. We have been uniquely blessed, yes, but we have never been uniquely God's only children! And our failure to come to grips with the incisive demand such a conviction draws out of us is the cause of much of the agony and criticism in relation to civil disobedience and demonstrations in America. Civil disobedience and other similar actions stand in the tradition of the prophets. Such action is steeped in a tradition verbalized by Peter and James: "We must obey God rather than man."

The attempt of Zephaniah to force Israel to abandon its isolationism and provincialism has relevance for the entire Christian church. Indeed, it has incisive insight for Southern Baptists. The church is looked upon by most of the dispossessed as a proper and stately bulwark against change. The radical message of Jesus has been transformed for so long into a comfortable homily, that Christians have been against life rather than thrust out into it. Jesus has been domesticated and enshrined behind a wall of outworn traditions. The congregation is often ruled by those whose high-handed dictatorial methods are the antithesis of what Jesus meant when he said, "He who would be greatest let him be servant of all."

So, the church is isolated and insulated from the agonies of the people about her by the very people whose initial confession involved a commitment to service. But this is rapidly changing. The church is moving toward others and their need. The church is becoming what Theodore Parker Ferris called "the church for others." This is why I believe the Southern Baptist Convention must abandon its traditional posture as provincial, and take up active and full participation in local, state, and national councils of churches.

The more we move in the direction of world want and need, the more apparent it will become that no denomination or communion alone has enough resources to make an impact on the problems which modern men face. Persistent racism which has been smoldering beneath the surface for so many generations broke out into the open and burned out the hearts of several cities in 1967. There is no way for the Christian church to face this problem divided into a hundred communions. Such a dilemma demands the total resources of the total Christian community. Southern Baptists had better forget the brush fires of discontent, admit their failures, and prepare for new strategies in overcoming the human problem of racism. We had better identify with all our Christian brothers in facing up to the problem. Let us move in the direction of identifying ourselves with those fighting for equal employment opportunities and dignity for the economically deprived. If we do not so identify ourselves we will be exiles in the land, walking among strangers who know us not. Zephaniah's pleas need not go unheeded in this day.

Let us never forget that the God who stands above the reach of men and who overshadows the history of every nation is the God of all men and that many of our actions have his condemnation rather than his approval. It is the business of the prophet to stand over against culture and over against nations to challenge them both. This was the stance of John Morley concerning Great Britain and the Boer War. He faced an antagonistic, indignant crowd one night in Manchester, England. Their fervor and patriotism had been whipped to a frenzy, but Morley still pleaded with his countrymen against the war. In part, he said this, "You may carry fire and sword into the midst of peace and industry. It will be wrong. A war of the strongest government in the world with untold wealth and inexhaustible reserves against this little republic will bring you no glory. It will be wrong. You may make thousands of women widows and thousands of children fatherless. It will be wrong. It may add a new province to your empire, but it will still be wrong." [1]

This man was standing in the prophetic stream, the same in which Zephaniah stood to castigate Israel and to promise her the destruction and devastation of God's judgment. He was unsparing in his prophetic denunciation. This is the reason I have called this sermon "Dark Is The Night." As far as the eye of this prophet could see there was the sin of

---

1. Quoted in Harry Emerson Fosdick's "The Church Must Go Beyond Modernism," *Riverside Sermons* (New York: Harper and Brothers, 1958), p. 362.

Israel standing out in stark contrast against his exalted view of God. Dark, indeed, was the night of Israel's sin and darker still would be the night of God's devouring judgment.

III. Streak of Light Against the Somber Night

In spite of Zephaniah's cry that the night of Israel's sinful disobedience is dark indeed, there is a restless stirring within the prophet's breast. Zephaniah appears to be the first of the "angry young men" who are so pessimistic about the structures of society that they can see no room for survival. It is difficult for Zephaniah to see any hope at all in the midst of the agony of Israel's disobedience and rebellion. Nevertheless, the prophet cracks open the door. There is the almost imperceptible streak of light against the dark and somber sky.

Isaiah's only reflection of hope was in his understanding of a new social order which encompassed a renewed and revitalized aristocracy. But Zephaniah's hope is that in a social order "the meek and humble" are submissive to God. To his mind the only hope for such a repentant, selfless remnant lay in the poor and oppressed. He saw no chance among the aristocratic—the proud arrogance of military kingdoms left little room for meekness and humility. They didn't want to be molded by the hand of God. They thought themselves self-sufficient and their pride and arrogance blinded them to whatever hope there was. "Dark was the night" of their pride and blind they were to the light.

When Zephaniah writes of meekness and humility he is setting his hope on those qualities of character which are most conducive to God's purpose among men. Meekness and humility are strengths not weaknesses. They belong to the person who has given up his pride and given himself to God so that a superior strength possesses him. It is the profound and creative strength of selflessness, freed from the tyranny of self-regard to live under the sway and dominance of God with a continuing openness to the invasion of God's graciousness.

Whatever hope there is for survival in this critical time is right here. Hope begins with this radical kind of integrity and character. This is the only thing that can overturn the world's repudiation of the value of persons. The creative strength of integrity both starts and maintains society's structures. People of this kind of radical integrity must be about the work of revolutionizing the fallacious institutions of society.

Zephaniah's word forces the desperate earnestness of life in upon us. We need to be reminded that the grace of God is just that—grace totally undeserved and given because God has withheld the judgment which is our due. In this there is our hope and in this there is our peace.

7. NAHUM

Man's Inhumanity to Man

Scripture: Nahum 1:11, 3:1–3, 3:19

There was a time in recent history when few people believed in sin. Early in the twentieth century there was such all-pervading optimism about human nature that sin was dismissed as an outmoded concept characteristic of an illiterate and unenlightened people. The initial days of this century were so alive with fresh discoveries, idealistic hopes, and alluring prospects that it was folly to waste much time with an ancient concept of human nature. Failures would be outgrown, dark ignorance would be illumined by education's light, and selfishness would be corrected by an era of prosperity and progress.

Twentieth-century man had good reasons for dismissing so readily the concept of sin. The scientific age had given birth to an inventiveness that filled human hearts with hope for man's abundant life. It looked as though a growing affluence would soon make available unlimited resources for the building of a new order of society and a better earth. The increasing use of electricity seemed to symbolize that the way to light the path of justice and brotherhood had been discovered. The science of refrigeration promised the time when massive structures, and perhaps even whole cities, would be comfortable from the heat, when foods would be preserved

74

indefinitely, and when the angry passions of men's hearts would be cooled infinitely. The achievement of swift transportation seemed to forecast a vast global community becoming a common humanity of brotherhood. Yet, "we invent airplanes and get bombers, invent automobiles and get tanks, explore chemistry and get incendiary bombs, create worldwide intercommunications and use them to produce blockades and famines. We blame our forefathers for even believing in infant damnation, but we, as it were, with our organized starvation and our bombing of cities, have taken over the job ourselves, using for our purposes the very gifts that were to have saved us. There is something demonic in human nature that can use the best for the worst." [1]

This gigantic delusion persevered until the outbreak of World War I, but with the resurrection of human nature's basic passions, the optimism of the age sank into oblivion as suddenly and abruptly as the *Titanic* when it struck that fateful iceberg. The horrid reality of sin as a deep-seated depravity in human nature could not be avoided. We know that there is something tragic and terrifying in human nature. It is something that turns our loveliest, most humane qualities to evil and sin and rebellion, that twists the finest part of man to the unholiest of ends.

The decade of the 1960s was a tragic and stark testimony to the reality of sin. Detroit, Newark, Watts, and Harlem are words that have become identical with the "summers of our American discontent." Rioting and plundering have become as common as the number of huge American cities. The smoldering ruins are a silent testimony to the sinfulness of man. The headlines of every day's newspaper scream their message to anyone who cares enough to listen. Strife between the nations, the murder of prominent public figures, the growing clamor of reactionaries to declare that the war against poverty has ended in failure—all these testify to the fact that man has a primitive, perverted, selfish pride which ruins

---

1. Harry Emerson Fosdick, *Living Under Tension* (New York: Harper and Brothers, 1941), pp. 113–14.

everything that man touches. Indeed, Robert Burns was correct when in his "Man Was Made to Mourn" he described history as the story of "man's inhumanity to man."

In many ways the twentieth century is similar to Nahum's time. The ancient world of Nahum's day was being shaken to its foundations. The nation Assyria was demonstrating the real truth of the phrase "man's inhumanity to man." Assyria was a nation of warriors whose chief delight was to plunder, ravish, and destroy.

I. Man's Inhumanity and Depravity

Nahum was a prophet-poet who lived just prior to the time of the fall of Nineveh in 612 B.C. His words seem clearly to be subsequent to Josiah's reformation of 621 B.C. There is no word of Judah's sin or unrighteousness and that can only be explained by the conditions prevailing after 621 B.C. Judah was now preeminently the people of God and the prophetic spirit had been codified and written into the statute book of the realm. Later it was possible for Jeremiah to see the hollowness and futility of the reforms, but Nahum was too close to the time the reform was initiated so that he had no opportunity to judge.

The weight of passion that charges the poetry of Nahum was provoked by the obvious brutality of the Assyrian empire.

With his own hand the king would gouge out the eye of noble captives or flay them alive and pin them to the ground to perish. Impalement of prisoners was a common practice. The Assyrian sculptures show us how the king could sit down to dine with the bleeding heads of captives hung around to give zest to his appetite. . . . He tore peoples from their homes and carried them far away until all patriotism was extinguished.

The Assyrian was a combination of the Roman and the Red Indian. His lawbook has been discovered recently and the penalties imposed in these laws are the most brutal of any in antiquity. Gouging out of eyes, hacking off the hands or other members of the body, cutting off the breasts of women, slitting the

nose, removal of ears, and pouring boiled tar over the head—
these are the things the Assyrian did.[2]

In our day we are guilty of this same kind of brutality.
Auschwitz and Lidice are parables of man's disdain for man.
If the prophet-poet Nahum were living in our day I am
sure that he would have acrid words for the kind of inhumanity to man that is being perpetrated by both the Viet
Cong and the American troops in Vietnam. It is an increasingly heavy burden for the American conscience to bear. And
when that situation is compounded by the riot situation in
the cities of the United States, you begin to wonder if the
strength of this American experiment is sufficient to permit
its survival.

I do not suggest that the troops of the United States are
more inhumane than the Viet Cong. There is abundant
evidence to make it clear that the Viet Cong are as rapacious
as any army in history. I mean to illustrate the kind of inhumanity that Nahum would condemn with a blistering
torrent of words, whether that inhumanity be perpetuated on
innocent people by either Americans or Viet Cong.

Nahum's ministry was directed against man's inhumanity
to man, and he came to this consuming passion and conviction
because he understood God to be the Lord of history. He assumed that God is the controller of the entire created order.
Nowhere did he delineate this fact explicitly, but it is a thread
which runs through the entire burden of his prophecy. Those
who would argue with this contention by saying that Nahum
was a narrowly nationalistic prophet are to be reminded of the
historical setting.

The reason Nahum had no condemnation for Judah is due
to the fact that serious social reforms were already on the
drawing boards. The reforms inspired by the teachings of the
prophets were given their impetus by the course events had
taken, and received their staging because of the sympathy of
the king and the people. "Accordingly, what we should ex-

---

2. John Paterson, *The Goodly Fellowship of the Prophets* (New York:
Scribner's, 1950), pp. 116–117.

pect the true prophet to have done would have been not to dwell on the past or present evils within the nation, but, seeing that Assyria's fall was not being brought about by intrigue and rebellion, to herald that coming event as the act of Jehovah, and in this way encourage Judah and her leaders in their work of reformation." [3] And the fact that his prophetic preaching took this precise form points to the strong belief he had in the universal sovereignty of God. Thus, Judah had responded to the disciplining wrath of God and no condemnation was deemed necessary. Rather, Nahum was true to the real prophetic spirit when the passion of his poetry is directed toward the brutality of the Assyrian regime.

II. A Diminishing Commitment to Service

At this point, Nahum has a live word for the church in the twentieth century. When we remember that the splendor of the great empires of history has crumbled into dust and ashes, and that this promise of decay is the message of history, we should also be reminded that our commitment to the service of all humanity has been diminishing. Unfortunately, it sometimes seems that the only lesson we can learn from history is that we learn nothing from history. The church can only persist to the extent it maintains and increases its commitment to God and to the world-wide community of mankind.

If we will but listen to the message of history, voiced by Nahum, we will be summoned back to the arena where man's inhumanity to man must be challenged with the purpose of God.

In November of 1967 W. W. Finlator, minister of the Pullen Memorial Baptist Church, Raleigh, North Carolina, sought to get his Baptist colleagues in North Carolina to challenge man's inhumanity to man in the arena of a state-wide meeting. He proposed, quite simply, that

---

3. G. G. V. Stonehouse, *The Books of the Prophets Zephaniah and Nahum, Westminster Commentaries,* ed. Walter Lock and D. C. Simpson (London: Methuen, 1929), p. 87.

Since the war in Vietnam not only threatens to continue the destruction of the people and resources of Vietnam and the youth and resources of the allied powers but also threatens a wider war and international peace and security, this war by the provisions of the Charter is subject to the jurisdiction of the United Nations.[4]

The North Carolina Baptist Convention should, he contended, recommend some proposals to the president and congress of the United States. Among these should be "the unconditional stopping of the bombing of North Vietnam for an indefinite period" and "the voluntary cessation of the killing and destruction in both North and South Vietnam with a cease-fire on land, sea and in the air. . . ." Here was an attempt to involve the church, the people of God, in a condemnation of the brutal slaughter of Vietnam's inhumanity to man and, as Finlator put it, "my fellow Baptists wouldn't even dignify it by sending it to the Resolutions Committee." What is Nahum's word at this point?

The message of Nahum should be a pause for a sobering reflection on our present course as a church and as a nation. The extent to which Nahum contains a note of militant nationalism may justify its secondary value in relation to other prophetic writings. Yet, the Christian church in America cannot fling the first stone. That same kind of nationalism, with a Christian overtone, is our subconscious religious faith in time of crisis. We have baptized our national purpose into the church. The refusal of the North Carolina Baptist Convention to speak to the Vietnam situation, under the guise that such action was beyond their ability to offer concrete proposals, is vivid evidence of this contention.

I remind you that the church will fail its mission when it becomes a mere culturally controlled institution. There is no way that the church can accommodate itself to the prevailing culture of any country. It is the destiny of the church and its role in America to stand over against blind nationalism and value-destroying cultural mores and challenge them.

---

4. Quotations taken from the proposal submitted to the North Carolina Baptist Convention by Dr. W. W. Finlator and used with his permission.

III. A Renewed Humility of Spirit

When one stands under the judgment of the God who is Lord of history, all arrogance and boasting disappear and, in their place, there appears that humility of spirit through which God can move. What has been misunderstood as a militant nationalism was, in reality, the recognition by Nahum that Jehovah is Lord of all human history. Let us, therefore, humble ourselves before Him that our continuing history shall be "his story" of redeeming grace working in us and through us for the healing of the brokenness of humanity.

In 1897, Rudyard Kipling was asked to write a poem celebrating the diamond jubilee of Queen Victoria. These were the days when the British Empire was a strong world power. The poem Kipling composed "baffled and angered many of his countrymen." [5]

Recessional

God of our fathers, known of old,
    Lord of our far-flung battle-line,
Beneath whose awful Hand we hold
    Dominion over palm and pine:
Lord God of Hosts, be with us yet,
Lest we forget—lest we forget!

The tumult and the shouting dies;
    The captains and the kings depart;
Still stands Thine ancient sacrifice,
    An humble and a contrite heart.
Lord God of Hosts, be with us yet,
Lest we forget—lest we forget!

Far-called, our navies melt away;
    On dune and headland sinks the fire.
Lo, all our pomp of yesterday
    Is one with Nineveh and Tyre!
Judge of the nations, spare us yet,
Lest we forget—lest we forget!

---

5. George A. Buttrick, ed. *The Interpreter's Bible,* vol. 6, pp. 957–58.

Let us never forget that He who is judge of the nations shall hold us responsible for our sin if we remain aloof from the brutalities of life. All the pathos and anger of a world awaits the announced word of redemption.

8. HABAKKUK
Wrestling with Life's Agonies

Scripture: Habakkuk 1:4, 1:13, 2:1–4

Anyone who is concerned with life's agonies and pains and who is wrestling with the problem of ultimate justice in our world will profit from taking the message of Habakkuk seriously. Those sensitive souls to whom the injustice of this created order is an increasing burden cannot avoid the issues that this prophet raises. Every observant and compassionate person is grappling with similar questions to these: Why should there be disease and suffering? Why should a child be born deficient physically or mentally? Why must the innocent suffer? Why are there earthquakes, tidal waves and devastating hurricanes? Why are there famines and slums and poverty? Why is there unemployment? Why is there rioting and looting in our cities? Why is there fighting and war?

In every generation of man's history these issues have plagued the sensitive conscience. Poets and writers have cursed heaven for the seeming idiocy and injustice of this universe. The book of Job is a voice railing against God because of the suffering and injustice visited on him. Florence Nightingale faced these questions when she wrote in her diary, "In my thirty-first year I saw nothing desirable but death." The Russian novelist and social reformer Leo Tolstoy experienced an unrelenting despair as he contemplated the issue of suffering in a universe of moral order.

The Scottish writer Thomas Carlyle has a dramatic passage in his strange book *Sartor Resartus* in which he muses about the age-long mysteries of suffering.[1] He has a character looking across the city at midnight. From an attic window he observes those dark streets and alleys where half a million human beings are crammed together in misery and hope. There they are "heaped and huddled together, with nothing between them but a little carpentry and masonry." They are alone with the stars of the vast, indifferent night. Even Jesus voiced his agony with the piercing cry from the cross, "My God, my God, why have you forsaken me?" He was wrestling with the same perplexing and bewildering problem. He was voicing an age-old question and finding the answer shrouded in an impenetrable mystery. There are those, today, who are suffering and they see misery as a slur upon divine providence.

Habakkuk initiates this interrogative mood in Israel's religious development and consciousness. For the first time, as far as Israel's history records, an inspired prophet is faced with the kind of situation which made some resolution of the problem a necessity. And he is forced to grope with the perplexing issue because of the particular and unique historical moment in time he occupied.

Amos and Isaiah and Micah and others had dwelt at length on the understanding of Israel's God as the one who acts justly and righteously toward his people. Amos had condemned any religious institutionalism which substitutes a cultus and ritual for integrity of character and justice in personal relationships. His renowned word, "Let justice roll down like waters, and righteousness like an everflowing stream," is not merely passionate oratory. It is a claim which God lays on his children. Isaiah of Jerusalem unfolded a vision of an exalted Lord whose universal purpose included a newly structured society in which the stability of a faithful, remnant people was the adhesive for a new order in a new

---

1. Quoted in James S. Stewart, *The Strong Name* (New York: Charles Scribner's Sons, 1941), p. 125.

age. This remnant would be moored so securely to a deep
and abiding commitment to God that apostasy would be an
impossibility. Micah preached a faith rooted in integrity of
character, nourished by sympathy and compassion of heart,
and sustained by a genuine reverence of spirit.

It is no surprising development, then, to hear the words of
Habakkuk as he seeks to relate the demanding claim of God
for personal righteousness to the nature of the created order
in which one lives and moves and has his being. Whether or
not Habakkuk was familiar with the writing of his prophetic
ancestors or of his contemporaries, is hard to say. But his
mind was troubled and his conscience quickened by the
same kind of conditions that aroused the sensitivity of the
prophetic spirit in others. Admittedly, he was moved in a
different direction, but this was because different historical
circumstances cry out for varying solutions. And these differ-
ing historical circumstances molded the reactions and forms
of action on which Habakkuk hung his prophetic burden.

The circumstances which inspired this prophet of God to
strike out against the ills of his day are not easily ascertain-
able. It is hard to determine the exact identification of "that
bitter and hasty nation" toward which his burden is directed.
In his opening chapter "the prophet draws a somber picture
of the grave social disorders of his day. Injustice and violence
reign supreme in the land. Tyranny and wrong triumph
everywhere. The wicked inflict merciless cruelty upon the
innocent. Men have become like the fishes of the sea, only to
be gathered into the dragnet of their despoilers. And these
oppressors of the people, the prophet observes ironically, not
only rejoice in their successes and exult in their triumphs,
but pay homage to their net. . . ." [2] So, conditions like these
posed an insurmountable difficulty for Habakkuk, for they
raised questions as to the righteous character of God.

I. An Abrasive Word

Against this backdrop of despair, all-pervasive and deep,

---

2. Israel Bettan, "Worshipping the Net," *Best Sermons, 1946* (New York:
Harper and Brothers, 1946), pp. 127–28.

Habakkuk offers an abrasive word against those social reforms which have no sustaining power behind them. The
quickening sense of hope that came with the reforms of
Josiah had submerged into domestic violence, internal strife
and contention. There was a slackening of emphasis on law
and order. Habakkuk's conscience forced him to the conviction that justice was being perverted. Civil disorder had dis-
placed the tranquility that was so characteristic of other days.

So the abrasive word which I see in the writings of
Habakkuk is that social reforms cannot hope to endure when
there is no sustaining moral power back of them. No matter
to what extent a fearless and indomitable reformer is able to
structure such reforms into the very fabric of our institutional
life they are doomed to inevitable failure unless there is an
effective moral foundation to support them. To be sure, social
reform begins with a sensitized conscience like that of Josiah.
But it will not hold its ground unless a vital and dynamic and
intelligent faith sustains it.

Harry Emerson Fosdick expresses it with a haunting para-
graph. He says that "going out with eager enthusiasm to save
the world, the launching of a ship is always a gala sight, with
flags and bands, bunting and cheering crowds. So you start
out on your expedition for a better society. But before that
ship comes to its last port it will face long-drawn-out storms,
howling northeasters, discouraging delays, and seas that
make the heart stand still. Such is the test of a mature
man's social hope. You are going to need a deep and patient
faith." [3] The sustaining power of a deep-rooted faith is an
absolutely necessary ingredient for the social reforms which
are being tried in this decade of the twentieth century.

You can seek to harmonize war and the demanding social
claim of the gospel; you can seek to rationalize the economic
inequities that produce the Harlems and the Watts, the
ghettos of every city; you can use every devious argument of
man to avoid dealing realistically with the poverty rampant

---

3. Harry Emerson Fosdick, *The Hope of the World* (New York: Harper and
Brothers, 1933), pp. 36–37.

in our country; you can use the old stereotypes of basic Negro inferiority to defend unequal employment practices and closed housing; but they will still be intolerable to a sensitive Christian conscience, and blasphemous before God. Therefore, the only alternative left is to seek to bring about reform, assuming that there is yet enough moral stamina left in our culture to sustain that reform before radical revolution takes over, and that those upon whom the burdens of our social inequities rest are still capable of patience. But even with this dual assumption as a live option, there is little hope this side of anarchy without the qualitative religious faith which redeems and transforms the inordinate self-will of unregenerate and arrogant men.

The fact that there is a social upheaval in the United States is no cause for alarm; on the contrary, it is a cause for elation. The disturbing facet of it is that it seems so far adrift from its moorings in a vital faith. I suppose that there is more truth than partisan criticism in the late Senator Everett Dirksen's remark that we need to be more concerned with building a good society than with an illusive dream of a great society. If that time is here when social reforms are free from their moorings then it may be too late for even radical social reforms.

Only a blind person could say that there is no need for reform. The inequities of our system have been so neglected that one wonders whether there is any surgery radical enough to treat them. This neglect has happened because of two fundamental problems that plague a free society. One is that honorable segment of society that can't see the despicable nature of our social ills. And, being free to direct and guide and influence the institutions of our free society, they have been able to abort social action programs. The other is that the social action programs which do come into being seldom reach responsible maturity because they drift away from their moorings—a sustaining supporting moral power.

Habakkuk's message calls us to that quality of repentance, faith, and commitment to God which will provide the moral foundations necessary for responsible social action. Without these there is little hope for either our free society or for the institutional structures of our common life.

II. An Impenetrable Mystery

A further prophetic word from Habakkuk concerns the impenetrable mystery of suffering and human agony. Judah, Habakkuk believed, was the people of God, and had a more intimate acquaintance with and relationship to God than any other nation. Therefore the people of Judah could reasonably expect protection from the military advances of heathen hordes; instead, they were being overrun by a ruthless oppressor, the Chaldeans. And because it was his theological understanding that suffering was the result of moral depravity, Habakkuk was deeply troubled.

Habakkuk had noted the disintegration which had begun to take place in the public morality. He had interpreted the advance of the Chaldeans as corrective discipline. But when that "bitter and hasty nation" swept across Judah with hasty cruelty and with a murderous contempt for God's people, the prophet paused to look again at the Chaldeans. They inflicted such outrage on their victims, were so violent in their covetous conquests, and were so ambitious and arrogant that the prophet began to reassess his evaluation of them. The Chaldean nation, which was first comprehended to be commissioned of God to humiliate transgressing Judah, turned out to be such a ruthless conqueror that even Habakkuk was surprised at the devastation wrought against Judah. "Not even Judah's personal sin and national transgression are grievous enough to provoke such wholesale slaughter and oppression of God's people," was Habakkuk's thought. "After all, they are still God's chosen nation and much more innocent in comparison with those wretched Chaldeans."

So the prophet is deeply distressed by the apparent injustice which prevails in the world. God's tolerance of injustice inflicted upon Judah is just unfathomable and bewildering. Trite and commonplace answers were to no avail for, in spite of them, the dark enigma of suffering was still utterly without light.

We must recognize that this is exactly what happens when the Christian faces his world realistically and candidly. The more sensitive the conscience to life's agonies, the greater the problem. The person whose commitment is boldly to God and to other people is the very one who has the "terrible task of squaring the dark, tragic things in life with a daring declaration of faith." [4] His sensitivity to God, his love and concern for all conditions of man, his joyous acceptance of his responsibility for the burdens of others—these are the very commitments which make him conscious of the fact that throughout life's fabric there runs a dark, tragic thread. Whereas one might logically expect the man of faith so to center his vision on the God of life and light to the exclusion of that dark thread, it is the sensitive conscience that finds his belief in God accentuates the problem of life's agonies.

III. A Steadfast Commitment

This leaves, as far as Habakkuk is concerned, only one other word to be said: the only real resolution of the problem is in the quality of one's steadfast commitment to God. "The righteous shall live by his faithfulness" (Hab. 2:4). By this the prophet is saying that man's concern cannot be to comprehend the impenetrable enigma or to explain the fact of suffering. As Habakkuk struggles with the mystery of human suffering, a fresh insight breaks in upon him. He concludes that the only solution to be discovered is inherent in his humanity. There is a sense of ultimate serenity that can come to any person of integrity who steadfastly lives as integrity dictates. Thus, for the prophet Habakkuk the interplay of his mind and conscience on the realities of God's providence, on man's sin and freedom, leads him to a solution in those qualities of the inner life which constitute the real man.

And for the Christian this quality of the human spirit is a creative response to God's extravagant graciousness in Jesus Christ. This response of openness liberates one's mind and

---

4. Stewart, op. cit., p. 129.

conscience from the debilitating factors at work in his experience and in his response to life's agonies about him. Then can come that serenity of the human spirit which enables one to face the raw realities of a world in travail, to participate in the pangs of that agony, and to lift the burdens of a suffering humanity up to God for redemption and release.

This response of openness comes in a critical moment of decision when one is faced with the utter despair and futility of his existence. Dr. H. H. Farmer writes movingly of what I mean. He says:

Many years ago as a young man I was preaching on the love of God; there was in the congregation an old Polish Jew who had been converted to the Christian faith. He came to me afterward and said: "You have no right to speak of the love of God until you have seen, as I have seen, a massacre of Jews in Poland—until you have seen, as I have seen, the blood of your dearest friends running in the gutters on a gray winter morning." I asked him later how it was that, having seen such a massacre, he had come to believe in the love of God. The answer he gave in effect was that the Christian gospel first began to lay hold on him because it bade him see God—the love of God—as it were, just where he was, just where he could not but always be in his thought and memories—in those bloodstained streets on that gray morning. It bade him see the love of God, not somewhere else, but in the midst of just that sort of thing, in the blood and agony of Calvary. He did at least know, he said, that this was a message that grappled with the facts; and then he went on to say something the sense of which I shall always remember though the words I have forgotten. He said, "As I looked at that man upon the cross, as I heard him pray . . . as I heard him cry in his anguish . . . I knew I was at a point of final crisis and decision in my life; I knew I must make up my mind once and for all, and either take my stand beside him and share in his undefeated faith in God—committing myself to the transcendent clarity of the vision of one so infinitely purer than myself—or else fall finally into a bottomless pit of bitterness, hatred, and unutterable despair.[5]

---

5. Herbert H. Farmer, *God and Men* (New York: Abingdon, 1947), pp. 190–91.

In this kind of a response of openness to God one is liberated from the brooding silence of humanity's agonies to a new quality of surrender to life's infectious serenity. And in the company of the Master there is renewed strength to wrestle with life's agonies and come from the struggle the victor!

9. JEREMIAH
Preaching an Uncomfortable Gospel

Scripture: Jeremiah 8:22–9:1

Someone has said that the role of the prophet is the twofold responsibility of "comforting the afflicted and afflicting the comfortable." This is no flippant, light view of the prophetic office. It says that, on the one hand, the prophet is to give himself to a healing ministry, drawing the bruised and wounded world into God's open arms. On the other hand, the prophet is to seek to bring a devastating word of judgment and indictment against man's self-righteousness, indifference, and unconcern. But if the prophet preaches one to the exclusion of the other, his ministry becomes unbalanced and a caricature of the gospel.

It is the role of the prophet to comfort those earnest and honest seekers who are continually overwhelmed with the daily frustrations of this maddeningly paced world. For them the transient, finite and meaningless round of routine has become a substitute for a life of quality that comes when God is at the center rather than on the circumference.

But the prophet whose only emphasis is on comfort contradicts the main tradition of Christian thought and life. Christian faith has never been chiefly comfortable. Rather, it is a style of life whose primary symbol is a cross. Christ had "no light-hearted view of life that let him stay, pleasantly drugged, in Nazareth, but a heavy-handed, serious view of life that caused him to walk at last the dark road to Golgotha." [1] Gandhi knew full well that one's religious commitment is no opiate. He said, "Jesus is the most exacting personage in the world and the world to come." History demonstrates the fact that India's great spirit took upon himself an uncomfortable burden. Gandhi could have lived out his days in a more peaceful and serene manner. However, he believed so deeply in God and his purpose for India that he was always on a demanding path. The fact of the matter was that God got Gandhi into trouble. He was gripped by the rigorous demand of an uncomfortable gospel.

And this brings us to Jeremiah. He found that his prophetic burden proved to be an uncomfortable gospel. His fidelity to the prophetic role forced him to lay emphasis on the afflicting side of the word from God. He refused to measure the success of his prophetic ministry by the general acceptance of his sermons; rather, he was committed, with an increasing dedication, to preaching that authentic word of God which was an uncomfortable gospel in his day.

Jeremiah's ministry is set in that period preceding the fall of Jerusalem. His family origins were noble and lofty and he was heir to a rich material and spiritual heritage. He was steeped in the finest Hebrew piety and nourished on its most meaningful traditions. In his day his land was being threatened by the forces of Nebuchadnezzar. The Babylonians were mobilizing to swoop down on Judah to destroy it. Every day they were inching closer and closer to the sacred city of Jerusalem. The future of the land of Israel was as dark and bleak as it had ever been and hope had reached the "nadir of nothingness."

And there was an equally dangerous threat within the nation. Once they had been a people with a resolute and overriding sense of divine purpose and destiny. But at the time of Jeremiah's ministry they had become fairly indiffer-

---

1. Harry Emerson Fosdick, *Riverside Sermons* (New York: Harper and Brothers, 1958), p. 105.

ent to the problems about them. The social and religious reforms which had been initiated under Josiah had been largely superficial. Although the altars erected to pagan gods had been destroyed and the Temple cultus had been re-instituted with a rigid adherence to its ritual, there was no fundamental improvement in the life of the people. Jeremiah was deeply disturbed by this situation. The prophet saw that the reform had merely replaced a crude form of idolatry with a more respectable, refined, and sophisticated form of idol-atry.

In the midst of this external threat and internal decay walked the prophet of God. It was his appointed role to preach the word of God faithfully in spite of all the blasé indifference. Because he would not preach a comfortable word, loneliness and ostracism were his lot. In him a dy-namic and challenging personality appears in the arena. And his book is written "with the lifeblood of a man, for in the case of Jeremiah, as in that of Hosea, the stream of relevation cut its channels deep into the experience of a suffering heart." [2]

I. Preaching for the Time's Predicament

The prophetic ministry of Jeremiah constrained him to walk "unflinchingly into the deepest defile of his time's pre-dicament. He looked into his time's abyss, and though there were moments when he recoiled from its terrors, he returned again and again to gaze more deeply until, beyond and beneath every anguish of his age, he discovered a new transcendent ground of hope." [3]

It was the time of Israel's demise as a historical and politi-cal entity, the period of Judah's final catastrophe. Jeremiah was hurled into "the time of great contention between com-peting world powers, and, with his people, stood in the midst of their vast collision. Not only was Judah a political bauble in the contending play of the great states but she was, as

2. John Paterson, *The Goodly Fellowship of the Prophets* (New York: Scribner's, 1950), p. 140.
3. George A. Buttrick, ed., *The Interpreter's Bible* (New York: Abingdon, 1956), vol. 5, p. 794.

Toynbee says, 'pounded on their native threshing-floor by an Assyrian flail.' " [4] Yet Jeremiah saw beyond these tensions that reality where God's purpose stands in judgment on history.

His first prophetic utterances had to do with the expected invasion of Judah by the dreaded Scythians. And when the anticipated peril failed to materialize, Jeremiah's standing as a prophet suffered irreparable damage. Later, as Jeremiah became more and more certain of the superficiality of the reforms initiated under Josiah, he condemned the people's superstitious trust in the Temple and delivered a sermon in which he predicted the Temple would be destroyed. Such an utterance so threatened the vocations of the priestly and prophetic groups who were part of the Temple cultus that they brought charges against Jeremiah. The way of safety was in reminding them that Micah had made the same prediction a century earlier.

Some years later, the prophet repeated the sermon, declaring the entire city of Jerusalem would be destroyed. This time Jeremiah was beaten and put in stocks. Undismayed by such treatment Jeremiah charged that all Jerusalem would go into captivity. As a further penalty, Jeremiah was denied entrance to the Temple court.

Because he was no longer permitted to preach in the Temple court, Jeremiah dictated his sermons to his secretary Baruch and told him to read them to the people at the next public feast. After Baruch had done this he was commanded to read the scroll to King Jehoiakim, son of Josiah. As the scroll was read to him, he cut it up, three or four columns at a time, threw it in the fire and ordered the arrest of Jeremiah and Baruch. Jeremiah redictated his messages and made additions to them.

By this time Babylon had become a world power and demanded tribute from the Hebrews. Jehoiakim refused to pay and Nebuchadnezzar marched to Jerusalem, laid siege to the city and took many captives. During the siege Jehoiakim

4. Ibid., pp. 794–95.

died and Zedekiah succeeded him. This last king of Judah was more favorably disposed toward Jeremiah but the war party bound his hands.

In spite of the people's belief in the inviolability of Jerusalem, Jeremiah declared that there was no way to turn back the judgment of God upon Judah; the only way to save the city of Jerusalem was to submit to the Babylonian king. This counsel was considered treasonous, so Jeremiah was arrested on the false charge of deserting to the enemy and was put into prison. But he continued his counsel of submission and so angered the administration that he was thrown into an empty cistern. Zedekiah refused the counsel of Jeremiah and continued to withhold tribute. So the Babylonians came to Judah again. This time the countryside was laid waste and after a siege of more than a year and a half, Jerusalem was devastated and burned. King Zedekiah was taken captive and many of the Jews were exiled.

A Jew named Gedaliah was appointed governor of Judah but, after five years, he was assassinated. Fearing reprisals from Babylon, many of the Jews fled to Egypt, forcing Jeremiah to go with them. Tradition has it that there he renewed his denunciation of the idolatry and was put to death by the exiled Hebrews. This is what I mean when I talk of the deep defile of the time's predicament.[5]

Through all the agony and travail of the time, Jeremiah moved with a divine sense of compulsion. Even though he felt that his was merely a rendezvous with doom, he never sought to avoid the prophetic ministry to his city and nation. John Watts' study of Jeremiah describes him well:

> Jeremiah showed deep spiritual insight and intense inner courage which was born of a struggle between his tendencies to weakness and the high calling of God. Forged in the bitter fires of personal experience, his words often reached a depth of personal intensity which can hardly be matched. He was lonely and isolated, a man who needed companionship and yet denied it to himself for the sake of the word of God. Jeremiah, like Hosea before him,

---

5. Buttrick, *op. cit.*, p. 778.

became an instrument through whom God showed the depth of his feelings for Israel. God's love, his grief, his despair, as well as his anger, were reflected in the corresponding emotions of the prophet.[6]

So, by this audacious commitment to what he understood to be his call from God, Jeremiah walked the jagged edge of the time's predicament and with a live word from God called men back to God.

II. A Personal Relationship to God

The ministry of Jeremiah speaks of that quickening word of a personal, covenantal relationship between the individual and God. During his ministry Jeremiah had witnessed the breakdown of the covenant God had made with the nation of Israel. He had had high hopes for the reform which Josiah had initiated. The covenant which was to have been the means for redeeming the nation had been abused and broken by arrogance and vanity. The people had deified the trappings of religion to the detriment of the heart of real religion. So Jeremiah began to talk of a new covenant which God would write on the heart.

By this Jeremiah meant that a person did not have to depend on a nation, a priest or a temple for his salvation. Some special dispensation of grace to those who were members of a favored community was not necessary. Rather, the individual stands alone before his God. "The ecclesiastical institution he will set aside or relegate to the background, for the pith and marrow of religion are not found there. The institution is external and impersonal, while religion consists essentially of a personal relation to the living God. Only as the springs of life are renewed can hope dawn for men. Grace must reign, for law has failed, and its failure is clearly seen. The religion of statute must give place to religion of the spirit, and the mechanical cult must give place to free and spontaneous worship." [7] In this thought the prophetic tradi-

6. John D. W. Watts, "Jeremiah—A Character Study," *Review and Expositor* vol. 58, no. 4, October, 1961, p. 431.

7. Paterson, *op. cit.*, p. 154.

tion of the Old Testament reaches a peak of insight.

Paterson writes of the personal, covenantal relationship of men with God in these words.

> Here religion bursts the bonds of nationality and takes on a universal aspect. Religion is made independent of time and place, and a new era is opened in the spiritual history of men. Nothing like this emerges in history until we come to the New Testament, and mark at Antioch the narrow walls of Jewish exclusiveness falling before the potent spirit of early Christianity. Religion is here conceived as personal communion with a personal God.[8]

The Church needs to be reminded of this magnificent insight.

III. A Condemnation of the Arrogance of Power

Jeremiah's ministry has another word of counsel for us in these critical days of the twentieth century—that we have a false sense of security. I feel certain that Jeremiah would have some prophetic utterances to direct toward that vanity and arrogance that is so characteristic of much of modern America. We have put our confidence in the wrong things.

In his day Jeremiah was deeply disturbed by what he saw. He saw his nation following a course of action which would inevitably lead to her utter ruin. With the enemy perched on the very borders of Judah, ready to swoop down on Jerusalem at the slightest provocation, Jeremiah counseled that the only course of action was surrender. If this counsel was refused, he said, then his country would fall to the Babylonians. "But no one seemed to care. The people thought they were safe in their multiple alliances, and Judah continued to follow those policies which would assure her destruction by powerful Babylonia." [9]

The relationships are parallel in only a very general sense between modern America and her enemies. The United States is undoubtedly more powerful than either the USSR or Red China. Even so, because of the infinite and unlimited

---

8. *Ibid.*
9. Corbett, *op. cit.*, p. 103.

power of nuclear explosives, another world war would bring disaster to the United States as well as to her enemies. Yet, it seems that the United States is bent on war with Red China in spite of anything anyone can do. The traditional forms of foreign policy are still being used even though two world wars attest to the fact that such methodology has been tried and found wanting.

I view Senator J. William Fulbright as a modern Jeremiah at this point. A recent address before the American Bar Association in Honolulu carries faint echoes of a Jeremiah. He said,

> . . . in this first era of human history in which man has acquired weapons which threaten his entire species with destruction, safety and prudence and realism require us to change the rules of a dangerous and discredited game, to try as we have never tried before to civilize and humanize international relations, not only for the sake of civilization and humanity but for the sake of survival.
>
> Even the most ardent advocates of an imperial role for the United States would probably agree that the proper objective of our foreign policy is the fostering of a world environment in which we can, with reasonable security, devote our main energies to the realization of the values of our own society. This does not require the adoption or imposition of these values on anybody, but it does require us so to conduct ourselves that our society does not seem hateful and repugnant to others.
>
> At the present much of the world is repelled by America and what America seems to stand for in the world. Both in our foreign affairs and in our domestic life we convey an image of violence; I do not care very much about images as distinguished from the things they reflect, but this image is rooted in reality. Abroad we are engaged in a savage and unsuccessful war against poor people in a small and backward nation. At home—largely because of the neglect resulting from twenty-five years of preoccupation with foreign involvements—our cities are exploding in violent protest against generations of social injustice. America, which only a few years ago seemed to the world to be a model of democracy and social justice, has become a symbol of violence and undisciplined power. . . .
>
> Far from building a safe world environment for American

values, our war in Vietnam and the domestic deterioration which it has aggravated are creating a most uncongenial world atmosphere for American ideas and values. The world has no need, in this age of nationalism and nuclear weapons, for a new imperial power, but there is a great need of moral leadership—by which I mean the leadership of decent example. That role could be ours but we have vacated the field, and all that has kept the Russians from filling it is their own lack of imagination.[10]

I can't know about you but I view these words as those of a Jeremiah. Of this one thing I am certain, if Jeremiah were alive and moving across the stage of twentieth-century American history, he would have some scathing words about what Fulbright called "the arrogance of power" in our country.

Stefan Zweig speaks graphically of the situation of Jeremiah's day and applies it to our day. In his drama *Jeremiah* he has two sentries on the walls of Jerusalem talking at night. "Do you hear that?" asks one sentry. "What is it?" comes the reply. "The sound is very faint, but the breeze bears it to us. When I was in Joppa, for the first time I heard in the night the distant murmur of the waves. Such a sound rises now from the plain. They are there in their thousands, moving quietly, but the air is stirred by the rolling wheels and the clashing arms. A whole nation must be afoot, falling upon Israel. The noise echoes from our walls like the noise of the sea. . . . Why does God hurl the nations against one another? There is room for all beneath the skies. There is still plenty of land unploughed; many forests still await the axe. Yet men turn their ploughshares into swords, and hew living flesh with their axes. I cannot understand." [11] Nor can I. When shall we learn that God holds us totally accountable for our violence and inhumanity against other men? So the word of judgment goes out and God's indictment is clear! Guilty! You have

---

10. J. W. Fulbright, "The Price of Empire," *Congressional Record*, vol. 113, no. 125, Washington, Wednesday, August 9, 1967, Senate Proceedings.

11. Quoted in *Interpreter's Bible*, vol. 5, p. 797.

rejected God's eternal covenants,
deleted sections of His commandments,
destroyed His binding agreements.

So God shall write a new covenant on your hearts with an indelible ink!

10. EZEKIEL

On Blaming the Watchman

Scripture: Ezekiel 33:1–6

To the prophet Ezekiel was given the task of rousing the spirits of his people in captivity in Babylon. The Hebrews were little interested in being revived, however. They were eight thousand families who had been uprooted from their homes by a ruthless invader and driven across seven hundred miles of desert into an alien land. After several years of imprisonment, word came back to their camp that the Babylonians had completely sacked Jerusalem, taken most of the inhabitants captive, and left their holy Temple a pile of rubble and ruin. Huddled in that foreign land, these Hebrews knew something of the fraternity of anguish. Any patriotic feeling that was left amongst them had to survive the brisk competition of an easy heathenism which had already lured many to accept the vices of Babylon and to forget the virtues of Zion.

Yet Ezekiel was determined that their spirit should be revived and resurrected. The continuing retreat of the Hebrews into an easygoing paganism was but goose-stepping to a funeral dirge, and he set for himself the harsh task of summoning them to a revitalized commitment to God. Ezekiel could see above the din and dust of time. He saw beyond the immediacy of the situation. He saw beyond their despair, and "if his feet were in the mud of unhappy circumstance, his forehead touched the shining stars of imperishable truth and splendor. His faith was firm, his hope a shining lamp, and God his greatest certainty." [1]

Ezekiel is the strangest figure of all the prophets. With bizarre ideas and grotesque imagery and apocalyptic forms his book presents itself as a volume of ancient riddles. Its complicated ideas and unfathomable mysteries lend themselves to those whom E. C. Rust calls the "crackpots of Christendom." And yet Ezekiel cannot be dismissed as a man subject to delusion or psychopathic experience or psychedelic trips. Ezekiel is thought to have been a member of the Zadokite priesthood. He was carried away to Babylon in 597 B.C. The evidence from his writings seems to indicate that he lived with the exiles but did not function as a priest in any official capacity. Four or five years later he received his inaugural vision, and his ministry extended past the time of the final devastation of Jerusalem.

I. Creativity Out of Exile

The first observation that I would make about the ministry of the prophet Ezekiel is that this time proves to be a constructive period of Hebrew history. It was a time when the scriptures were written down and canonized, when sacred traditions were codified, when the history of Israel was recorded in some acceptable form, and when steps were taken to prepare for the future.

"The exile contributed much to the historical development of Judaism, and at its beginning stands Ezekiel. To the exiles at first there was present only the thought of loss and desolation. But the exile was not all loss. Babylon was a great city and Nippur was of high antiquity, and here there was a cultural tradition longer than any Israel had ever known. The Jews could not live there without, in some measure, sharing

---

1. Hobart D. McKeehan, "Deathless Dreams," *Best Sermons, 1944,* ed. G. Paul Butler (Chicago: Ziff-Davis, 1944), p. 358.

that tradition." [2] Indeed, the exile was a fruitful and a creative time.

And there is truth for us here if we have the sensitivity to open up to it. The most natural and human reaction to such a time of trouble is to rebel against it and to refuse to use it as a creative experience. Although the accumulated insight of man's history teaches us to use such a time to allow good to come, we just are not able. When trouble comes into our experience we see it as an invasion. Instead, we should see it as a time to bring some creative insight to us.

Harry Emerson Fosdick writes of Marie Antoinette's experience in learning this lesson. "Marie Antoinette added the final stroke of levity and folly which ruined the old regime and brought on the bloody terrors of the Revolution. A silly, frivolous girl, grace and charm personified, she flitted amid the pleasures of Versailles or fooled with her favorites at the Little Trianon. But when at last the Revolution broke and all her world of tinsel playthings came collapsing down and she faced calamity and death, she turned out to be a strong, courageous woman. Character had been underneath there all the time. Versailles never had released her depths. It took catastrophe to bring them forth." [3] This is exactly the thrust of what Paul meant when he wrote, "God works in all things for good unto those who are called according to his purpose."

And because the Hebrews were able to look creatively over the meaning of their experience in Babylon, history attests to the fact that they returned from the exile a people of God in whose hands God had laid a unique destiny. And if anyone had been given a ready alibi for giving in and cracking up and despairing, that man was the prophet Ezekiel. He was in what appeared to be a crazy and hopeless situation. He had hours of self-pity in which he saw nothing beyond the limited horizon of his own feelings. He had hours of such bewilderment that he couldn't even determine what step to take next.

---

2. Paterson, *The Goodly Fellowship of the Prophets* (New York: Scribner's, 1950), p. 164.

3. Harry Emerson Fosdick, *The Secret of Victorious Living* (New York: Harper, 1934), pp. 11–12.

He had every temptation to quit and give up. But, somehow, he responded to God's summons and became a sentinel set to call Israel to God.

"Ezekiel was one of these unconquerable souls. Indeed, it is not impossible that but for Ezekiel there had been no Second Isaiah. More than any other one man, Ezekiel assured the continuance of the faith of Israel in the alien land, and for that matter for centuries afterwards, since he is rightly called 'the Father of Judaism'. . . . He and his companions were plunged into an abyss so deep that most of them could see nothing but the darkness and the restricting walls. But Ezekiel looked in a different direction: *he looked up,* and he saw the otherwise invisible stars." [4]

And a difficult situation can call out of us a new power and a new spirit, capacities and abilities that no fair-weather situation can ever command. When we face our Babylonian captivities we can find new strengths to face the ills with an undaunted courage. If my memory serves me correctly it was Joseph R. Sizoo who said he liked to remember that the great civilizations of history were born and nourished by the rigors of the Northern Hemisphere. It is not in the temperate and equatorial zones but in the brisk atmosphere of the northern zones. When life is comfortable and easy then there is no record of lasting achievement. This is exactly the lesson of these exiles and their prophet Ezekiel.

II. Individual Responsibility—"Life Is Reversible"

In the second place, I would speak of the nature and quality of the prophetic leadership that Ezekiel gave to these exiles. The significance of Ezekiel 33 is to be found on this level. Ezekiel uses the symbol of the watchman who stands guard. He is responsible for sounding the alarm if danger or foe comes. This places a great responsibility on the watchman. If he fails in his task he is punished with death. But his responsibility ends when he has fulfilled his duty. If the people

---

4. Edwin Lewis, "The Song of the Exiled," *Best Sermons, 1947,* G. Paul Butler, ed. (New York: Harper and Brothers, 1947), pp. 28–29.

do not heed the clearly sounded warning, that is their responsibility, not his. As a prophet, Ezekiel knows his obligation to warn the nation against doing evil and accepts his responsibility very seriously, but he sets a clearly defined and ethically sensible limit to his duty.

By almost all of our normal criteria Ezekiel is the sensible leader. No man can reasonably be expected to do more than he proposes to do. The way in which a people respond to the words of prophetic admonition is quite beyond the control of the prophet. It would be grossly unjust to hold a man responsible for what other men do. Nobody would become a leader if his own record were made hostage to the behavior he engendered in those to whom he preached.[5]

And, yet, when the responsibility is put where it obviously belongs we are able to hear that kind of truth. Articulately expressed in Ezekiel is the doctrine of an individual responsibility. It is the obligation of every individual to respond to whatever light he may have. We need this truth to be heard afresh today.

I am conscious of the fact that environment and heredity have an influence on what a person becomes. And much of the time I am convinced that the influence of the environment is so strong that very little of life is reversible. This, I suspect, would be the major reason for rooting out the slum environments of many places in our nation. Psychiatry and sociology tell us that it is necessary to understand how a person was influenced in his formative years if you are to understand his present reactions to crisis matters. This is true, but, at the same time, the fact is that we are responsible for our actions. There is no way to escape this.

Yet, what do we do? Do we accept the responsibility for a course of action that caused ruin and trouble in our lives? Do we admit the fact that we stubbornly chose a path that led in a different direction than we intended? Do we confess to the truth that we boarded the wrong bus and thereby

---

5. Edward LeRoy Long, Jr., "Goodness and Grace," *The Pulpit*, January, 1964, pp. 4-6.

arrived at a wrong destination? Or do we try to rationalize and attempt to elude and evade responsibility.

I have called this sermon "On Blaming the Watchman." The symbol is lifted straight from the prophecy of Ezekiel. The prophetic watchman deserves to be blamed if he fails to warn the people of a given danger. But it is often the case that the people hear the warning, do nothing about it, and then blame the watchman. And blaming the watchman for their own failure is to violate all the canons of good sense.

III. Social Responsibility

Ezekiel not only taught individual responsibility, he stressed social responsibility. Ezekiel questioned the traditional theology of the Hebrews—the dependence on the solidarity of the community for acceptance by God. This teaching had a meaningful place in the development of Hebrew religious thought. But every generation since the proclamation of the Abrahamic covenant had added its accretions to the commonly accepted principle of the covenant. What was by Ezekiel's day orthodox Hebrew thought was a perversion of Hebrew theology. What had originated as a covenant of responsibility had degenerated to an expression of particular privileges and nationalism. Therefore, when Ezekiel asserted that the reservoir of their national heritage had become polluted by a self-asserting pride and that the only hope for them was the obligation of personal righteousness, he opened windows through which freshness could move into the Hebrew consciousness.

Ezekiel incisively slashes through the assertions adhering to covenant theology and arrives at the very heart of the matter, man's individual responsibility before God. What had been initiated in the framework of humble servanthood had become a concept of vaunted privilege, and authentic religion as voiced through Ezekiel condemned this concept as insufficient.

Yet, Ezekiel's emphasis on individual responsibility is not without its limitations. Every man is responsible for himself and for the decisions he makes. He cannot deny or evade or escape the fact of his responsibility for molding and shaping and guiding his own destiny. Still, this is no avenue for his final escape from social responsibility. Ezekiel wrote of individualism in a concerted attempt to break the high-handed attitude of those who felt their corporate security rested on a convenantal basis. He contended that traditional Hebrew marketplace theology had provided an avenue for them to escape personal responsibility for the sins of the nation. But, there is no such absolution of guilt to be found, the prophet asserts.

So the truth comes surging in on us at this very interval. We, too, are guilty of trying to avoid responsibility for the social ills that plague this twentieth-century world. We try to place the blame for the social inequities of our time on government, on irresponsible agitators, on outsiders and on communists. We refuse to admit our complicity in the situation. So we make the H. Rap Browns and the Stokeley Carmichaels our scapegoats. We blame the riots on professional radicals. This makes it easier to justify one's refusal to accept his share of the responsibility for the Watts and the Newarks and the Detroits.

It would be pushing Ezekiel's picture too far to suggest that his word for us is directly related to this human propensity to evade responsibility for social problems. But it is a relevant interpretation of his prophetic burden to move in this direction. This evasion takes many forms. One of the most prominent forms is that of church activist. He avoids the stab of the gospel by listening for the squeaks in the institutional machinery of the church. He avoids the call to involvement by insisting on polite and sedate sermons on the nature of the heavenly city and being indifferent to the secular city of man's poverty, unemployment, job and housing discrimination, and exploding ghettos. He avoids the prophetic condemnation of militarism parading in the guise of patriotism by the folly of his insistence that church and state must be kept separate.

Ezekiel forces us to an alarming confrontation of ourselves. But he could do it because he knew Israel was strong only when she forgot the agony of her captivity and looked to Israel's God. God's purpose for Israel had not reached a dead end. Their tragic situation in Babylon was not the final word. Their experience was but a crucible from which God would bring a people purged and chastened and fit to be his renewed people for the coming new age.

There is another side to the social implications of Ezekiel. Mere proclamation is not enough. Ezekiel's emphasis on individual responsibility was a needed corrective and a healthy abrasive for a people who counted on a corporate solidarity for their deliverance. Nor did Ezekiel intend his call to individual responsibility to be opposed to social involvement. But the interpretation of Ezekiel's emphasis has led to the inevitable conclusion that verbal enunciation of truth is enough to elicit change. His image of a watchman standing guard, ready to sound the alarm, needs to be balanced with involvement in correcting the sins of the nation. In the total context of prophetic religion this tension is maintained. Therefore, this simple warning is sufficient.

The church needs to face this truth candidly. Reconciliation, forgiveness, and acceptance come not through the mere enunciation of their availability. These truths continue to be elusive realities until such time as the issue is joined. Forgiveness and reconciliation come through agony and suffering, just as Hosea contended. Human institutions are usually impervious to change until they are forced to introversion by demonstrations of unjustified suffering. The reason Martin Luther King has become a household word is because he captured this truth and used its power to challenge the moral conscience of the nation. The drama of Bull Conners' police using cattle prods against the Negro demonstrators thrust a mortal wound to the body of a segregationist way of life that, even then, was writhing in the throes of its final agony. Involvement complemented and brought to fruition an enunciated truth.

So I conclude with a call to the church to get out of its comfortable sanctuaries into the thick of the bruising battles of life. As John Gardner, formerly Secretary of Department of Health, Education and Welfare, observed in a recent speech, "This is a day of dissent, divisiveness; everyone speaks with unbridled anger in behalf of his point of view for his party, his people. But the fissures in our society are already dangerously deep. We need greater emphasis on the values that hold us together."

Yes, there is a profound discontent with those social ills which are perverting and distorting and poisoning the fundamental idea which is America. So the call I am issuing is for the church to use its total resources for binding up the wounds of men. This will mean that the church will know the pain of conflict. But above all, the church will know the serenity that comes because it has wrestled with anger until it yielded mercy.

The local church must become a "congregation that is struggling to learn now to love the world with risk, a congregation that will tolerate nothing short of a free pulpit, a congregation with maturity to sustain and embrace and transform all the antagonisms of society, a congregation that gives a thousand tongues to sing God's grace and praise not only with their lips but with their lives as well." Every local congregation must become the means through which God's love becomes healing balm for every beaten and wounded pilgrim. In short, the church must speak in "ever fresh and new ways to embody, to dramatize, to share, to give God's mercy in the city." [6] And there is no way to escape your responsibility for such action. You can "blame the watchman" who has sounded the alarm, but the burden of caring will still be yours to bear!

---

6. Robert A. Raines, "The Missionary Congregation in the Secular City," unpublished sermon, p. 6. Used by permission.

11. OBADIAH

Mankind's Deepest Treason

Scripture: Obadiah 1:2–3, 15, 18, 21b

Benito Mussolini wrote in his *Autobiography:* "I do not drink; I do not smoke; and I am not interested in cards or games. . . . As for the love of the table, I don't appreciate it. . . . In every hour of my life it is the spiritual element which leads me on. . . . I have annihilated in myself every egoism. . . . I feel that all Italians understand and love me; I know that only he is loved who leads without weakness, without deviation, and with disinterested and full faith." Mussolini may have thought he had annihilated in himself every egoism—but he did not know that that is an impossible task. Pride is the most subtle and the most devastating of human sins.

The church is also subject to the temptation of pride. There is no sorrier spectacle than a congregation which has succumbed to pride. The temptation comes to a congregation when it begins to see itself from the viewpoint of its tradition and heritage. The next step is to view itself as the preserver of those traditional values. Then it is only little removed from seeing itself as a proud, exclusive, and strong bulwark against social change. Patronizing and paternalistic attitudes toward the dispossessed and culturally deprived are, then, the usual case. Socially, the congregation becomes a self-perpetuating expression of one class of society. And, finally, this degenerates into a congregation that cares little about persons, that has little dynamic and creative concern, and that has lost its courageous heart.[1] Indeed, Sinclair Lewis's Babbitt would be at home in that congregation that has forgotten its mission, that caters to wealth, and that has become a reflection of all middle-class values.

Such a stance by any church is blasphemous, contrary to the New Testament teachings about the church, contradictory to the missionary stance of the evangelical Protestant church, and an utter and flagrant denial of the life and spirit of Jesus. And, yet such a stance is more characteristic and widespread than many of us are ready to admit. In many parts of American society the church has become an institution to preserve the religious ceremonies of a semi-Christian and semi-pagan culture.

If you were to take a cross section of the average church in America and analyze it, and if you were to take a cross section of the typical nonchurchgoing populace and analyze that, I feel certain that honesty and candor would force you to admit that it is extremely difficult, yes well-nigh impossible, to distinguish which is "Christian" and which is "secular." In much of modern society the church would be hard-put to demonstrate that its presence in a given community has made any real difference in the quality of the corporate life.

Such a viewpoint is not without its documentation and its testimonials. It can be substantiated by reference to numerous sources. Sociologist Peter Berger writes about it. "The most common delusion . . . is the conviction of ministers that what they preach on Sunday has a direct influence on what their listeners do on Monday." [2] Foy Valentine writes, "The modern world neither experiences our naked power nor encounters the thrust of our moral strength, as it did when Christians were, though despised and rejected, still sure of

---

1. For an incisive picture of what happens when a congregation does succumb see Wallace Fisher's *From Tradition To Mission* (New York: Abingdon, 1965), pp. 25–35.

2. Peter L. Berger, *The Noise of Solemn Assemblies* (Garden City: Doubleday, 1961), p. 37.

the rightness of their cause." [3] Pierre Berton says, "Institutional Christianity, in short, has become a comfortable creed, a useful tool for Peace of Mind and Positive Thinking, a kind of sugar-coated pill that soothes those who fear to face the traditional Christian concerns of evil, suffering, and death—concerns, be it said, that have been miraculously minimized and glossed over by the religious establishment." [4] So the ultimate end of pride is the utter annihilation of the distinguishing marks of that quality of life which is called Christian.

I am convinced that the heart of the matter is this arrogant, self-seeking spirit of man that is called pride. Theologians call it sin. L. H. Marshall calls it "inordinate self-love"; [5] Paul Tillich calls it "a denial of finitude"; [6] Karl Barth calls it "rebellion and violation of the ordinance of his existence"; [7] Emil Brunner calls it "rebellion against and defiance of God"; [8] the Bible calls it rebellion, missing the mark, or transgression. But regardless of what you call it, it is an arrogance of spirit, a self-asserting pride, an ostentatious and contentious heart, and a vanity of life. This is the kind of arrogant, self-concerned spirit against which the prophet Obadiah writes.

The prophet Obadiah is as obscure an individual as you will encounter in the Bible. He is virtually an unknown. Some have tried to identify him with the servant who cared for some one hundred prophets in the days of Ahab. Others have sought to identify him with King Ahaziah's captain, but he still maintains a self-imposed anonymity. Some scholars believe that Obadiah was "too much concerned with

3. Foy Valentine, *The Cross In The Marketplace* (Waco: Word Books, 1966), p. 50.
4. Pierre Berton, *The Comfortable Pew* (Philadelphia: Lippincott, 1965), p. 82.
5. L. H. Marshall, *The Challenge of New Testament Ethics* (London: Macmillan, 1947), p. 32.
6. Paul Tillich, *The Protestant Era* (London: Nisbett, 1951), pp. 241–43.
7. Karl Barth, *The Knowledge of God and The Service of God* (London: Hodder, 1949), p. 47.
8. Emil Brunner, *The Christian Doctrine of Creation and Redemption* (Philadelphia: Westminster, 1952), pp. 92–93.

his prophetic task to think of his own personal identity or his literary fame," [9] but such a position is somewhat antithetical to the reflection of the man which you find in his brief writing.

Although controversy has raged around this book in regard to its integrity and although it is almost universally accepted that the final verses are from a later period, I shall be treating the writing as a meaningful whole as far as its message is concerned. And, immediately, it should be noted that this prophetic burden has its rootage in a family squabble, in the controversies between Jacob and Esau. Throughout Israelite history there was a feud between Israel and Edom. It was further aggravated by the decision of Edom to refuse Moses and the Israelites permission to travel across his territory when they were in flight from the slavery and bondage of Egypt. They were forced to take their journey around Edom. But the final straw was a result of the position Edom took relative to the Chaldean advances against Jerusalem. The Chaldeans capitalized on the hostility and invited Edom to become an ally as they laid siege to the Holy City. So the historical circumstances which make possible the most feasible interpretation of this tirade against Edom are related to this final siege of Jerusalem. During the decade that followed the fall of Jerusalem in 587 b.c., Obadiah pens his brief and pointed book.

I. The Root of Hostility

The first truth that comes surging out of Obadiah is that inordinate self-concern and pride stir hatred and hostility in the human family, and therefore this hateful and arrogant spirit is mankind's deepest treason. The Old Testament has many examples of such imprecatory denunciations of foreign nations and peoples, but none equals the hostility of Obadiah's passion against Edom. Through the prophet Obadiah, Israel casts her fiercest and bitterest venom. "Brutus' act to Antony was treachery to friendship but this was a

---

9. John Paterson, *The Goodly Fellowship of the Prophets* (New York: Scribner's, 1950), p. 179.

denial of the covenant of brotherhood." [10] Obadiah maintains that Edom's treasonous action against Israel would never be forgotten or erased from the minds of the people. He writes,

> But you should not have gloated
>   over the day of your brother
> in the day of his misfortune;
> you should not have rejoiced over the people of Judah
>   in the day of their ruin;
> you should not have boasted
>   in the day of distress.
> You should not have entered the gate of my people
>   in the day of his calamity;
> you should not have gloated over his disaster
>   in the day of his calamity;
> you should not have looted his goods
>   in the day of his calamity.
> You should not have stood at the parting of the ways
>   to cast off his fugitives;
> you should not have delivered up his survivors
>   in the day of distress.
>
> For the day of the Lord is near upon all the nations.
> As you have done, it shall be done to you,
>   your deeds shall return on your own head.
>   —Obadiah 1:12–15 RSV

So the denial of the covenant of brotherhood by Edom is to be condemned as a part of mankind's deepest treason.

This small pamphlet was written out of the bitterness and soreness of defeat. Judah had fallen. As the prophet looked at the smashed lives of his people, he was stung to the quick. It was not the thought of aliens lolling in their former homes. It was not the desecration and pollution of the holy places by a heathen people that bothered him. It was the callous indifference and cool unconcern with which their kinsmen, the Edomites, had watched their struggle. They had fought for their lives as the Chaldeans stormed Jerusalem,

---

10. Paterson, *op. cit.*, p. 185.

but the Edomites stood by in their inaccessible mountain fortress and did nothing. So the fury of Obadiah rolled and crackled like some reverberating thunderstorm.[11] The Edomites had refused to honor the covenant of kinship with Judah, and Obadiah unleashed a torrent of hostility against them. "Your open indifference is treason," cries Obadiah. Indifference on the part of Edom bred hatred and animosity in Israel.

Such hostility and animosity in any part of the human family breeds the inevitable frustrations of pride, arrogance, rebellion, and self-concern. And in such a spirit there is the inherent inability to organize any form of the common life. Such a spirit frustrates because that person is not satisfied with a real acceptance of his own personhood with all its finite limitations. There is a reciprocity of pride and arrogance, on the one hand, and hostility and hatred, on the other.

For the Israelite, Edom represented that proud, haughty, arrogant spirit that maintains confidence only in itself. For Edom, Israel represented an unfounded and ungracious hatred and hostility. Therein is the story of their unrelenting hatred for one another. There is something structured into the very nature of human life that resists the haughty and proud. And the paradox of the matter is that such pride and arrogance are universally unfounded.

> I love to watch the rooster crow.
> He's like so many men I know,
> Who brag and bluster, rant and shout,
> And beat their manly chests without
> The first darn thing to brag about.[12]

I could hope that this modern world in which we live could learn a few elementary facts at this point, but it seems impossible. Even though this prophetic burden teaches that "hate silences the voice of compassion, blinds the soul's vision, corrupts the social fabric," we continue the wars that

---

11. Arthur John Gossip, *The Hero in Thy Soul* (New York: Scribner's, 1933), pp. 172–73.
12. Author unknown.

blight mankind with their hatred and folly. We continue inflicting agonies in the name of a "defense of freedom." We continue our arrogant pose as the world's moral leader, trying to inflict the rest of the world with our Western values, values which have lost much of their magnetism because they are not now producing a way of life that is obviously superior to that of the rest of humanity. When are we going to learn that such inordinate pride stirs up hatred and hostility in the human family and thereby is mankind's deepest treason?

II. The Human Character of the Bible

Another live word emerges from Obadiah and that is the fact of the very human nature of the Bible. When you first read this harangue against Edom you wonder how it ever got into the canon. Then, if you read the Gospel of John in conjunction with your study of Obadiah the contrast is markedly more striking. One is a high-water mark of revelation and the other appears to be one of the least significant books of the Bible. Then you can begin to see why G. A. Studdert-Kennedy likened reading the Bible to a jumble sale where "you can get anything from an antediluvian umbrella to a priceless print."

Does this mean that the church's teaching concerning the inspiration of the Bible is false? Absolutely not! It simply means that the truth of that teaching has been misunderstood. The Bible's claim is that it was written by inspired men.[13] Much of the talk about an *inspired Bible* is not comprehensive enough to embrace all that is meant. It uses a phrase relating to the realm of life, not of inanimate objects. Saying that the Bible is "inspired," veils the fact that the Bible was written by "inspired writers."

The point is that the Bible is a vehicle which seeks to convey the mighty acts of God in human history. It is the story of God's self-disclosure of his loving mercy and gracious redemption. It is written by men whose commitment to the God of the present and the beyond empowered them for their

---

13. 2 Peter 1:21.

struggle with the dark riddle of human existence. And through these inspired men, God seeks to move toward all men with a word that comes alive with a fresh vitality in every generation. Through frail men God speaks of his rigorous demands for love not servility, for goodness not cultus, and for loyal obedience not just docile worship at a shrine.

After all is said and done, it is this very human character of the Bible that is its attraction. It is the lively word of God just because it is a very human instrument that God uses to reach men. A divine book filled only with the gallant, perfect deeds of deity would hold little attraction for us. Rather than being its Achilles' heel, the human character of the Bible is its magnetism. Studdert-Kennedy says it well:

> Part of men's discontent with the Bible, like their discontent with the universe, is due to the fact that they have at the back of their minds the ancient misconception of an absolutely almighty being who can do anything he chooses. They think just as God spoke the word and the stars came out, spoke yet again and the flowers grew, waved His wand and made a universe, as Cinderella's Fairy Godmother made coaches out of pumpkins, so that Almighty God has nothing else to do but touch men's lips and from their mouths perfect truth in perfect words will flow like golden rivers.[14]

But, because God inspired men, rebellious, stubborn, sinful, and self-willed men, to write as they were moved, the Bible speaks to our condition today. The difficulty with the preaching and teaching of the Bible is that we have so removed it from our human experience that it is easy to dismiss it as an impossible demand.

III. Jesus' Humanity His Attraction

This is exactly what we have done with Jesus Christ. We have crucified the humanity of Jesus on the cross of his divinity and, by so doing, we have removed him and his rigorous ethical demand from the realm of our human experience. After all, it is easier to live with such a view of

---

14. G. A. Studdert-Kennedy, *Lies!* (London: Hodder, 1919), p. 194.

Christ. We can worship him and at the same time dismiss his moral insights and ethical demands. This is what Harry Emerson Fosdick meant in his sermon "The Peril of Worshipping Jesus." He wrote,

> Throughout history it has been true that when a spiritual leader has been too powerful to be crushed by opposition there has been still another way to escape his moral insights and his ethical demands, and that is to worship him, hide his too-piercing eyes in the smoke of sacramental adoration, build beautiful sanctuaries where his challenging social ideals may fade out in vague mysticism, get him off somewhere on a high altar, pray to him, sing to him, do anything for him rather than let him get back again where he started, walking the common ways of men and talking about how to live—that always had been the most successful way of getting rid of Jesus.[15]

This is the one way of getting rid of the demand of the Bible and the demand of Jesus. This removes the Bible from the realm of our experience. This makes the Bible so supranatural that there is no reason for us to measure the quality of our living by its divine and elevated and impossible demand.

IV. The Hope of the Larger Purpose of God

Emerging from the travail of Judah's agony and out of the devastation which Edom actively perpetuated against Judah a glimmer of light does break. It was a ray of hope which the prophecy of Obadiah cast against the night of Judah's destruction. It seems to be a note appended by another hand, yet it stands as a fitting climax to Obadiah's message.

Lanchester puts it like this, "The prophet seems for a moment to be transported beyond the sphere of rivalry and cruelty and suffering, and to realize that all that has been happening, and all the future consequences of it, will in due time lead on to the establishment of the kingdom of the

---

15. Harry Emerson Fosdick, *The Hope of the World* (New York: Harper, 1933), p. 96.

Lord." [16] So this hymn that both represents and condemns mankind's deepest treason points, finally, to the large light of the purpose of God. Hostility and animosity are to be absorbed in the larger light of the way of love and mercy and forgiveness.

It was the darkest day in all of Israel's history. The Temple had been destroyed, the beloved city lay in ruins and the people had been sent into exile. The mocking hordes of foreigners surged over the land. Obadiah was a Jew who had lived through all the travesties of both Edom and Chaldea. He had passed from the city of ruins with the sound of mocking laughter ringing in his ears. Yet, he dared to fling back into the teeth of the conqueror the burden of this book. "Our day is not over. We shall yet return and take the land. The land will belong to us again and the kingdom shall be God's."

And I reply from the vantage point of the twentieth century. "O, thou courageous and dauntless heart! The exile will chasten you so that you can serve this secular world. The narrow rule of Israel shall be no more. And after years of exile you shall be fitted to become servant of the whole community of mankind. Only then will the deepest treason of your pride and rebellion be swallowed up by the triumphant, abiding purpose of God in history."

16. H. C. O. Lanchester, "Obadiah and Jonah," *The Cambridge Bible for Schools and Colleges* (Cambridge: University Press, 1915), p. 35.

12. ISAIAH OF THE EXILE
Servant of His Eternal Purpose

Scripture: Isaiah 42:1–7

In the last twenty-five or thirty years, there have been several great men who have captured the public imagination. Winston Churchill was one of these. His great spirit struck fire in the hearts of Englishmen as they struggled against Hitler's military might. On July 14, 1940, he captivated the imagination of the world with his sobering speech: "Bearing ourselves humbly before God but conscious that we serve an unfolding purpose, we are ready to defend our native land against the invasion by which it is threatened. We are fighting by ourselves alone. But we are not fighting for ourselves alone. . . . Should the invader come to Britain, there will be no placid lying down of the people in submission before them. . . . We shall defend every village, every town, and every city . . . ; we would rather see London in ruins and ashes than that it should be tamely and abjectly enslaved. . . . Thus only, in times like these, can nations preserve their freedom." [1]

In the sixties John F. Kennedy captured the world's imagination as no recent American president has been able to

---

1. Quoted in F. Lee Benns, *European History Since 1870* (New York: Appleton-Century-Crofts, Inc., 1950), p. 680.

do. He had a commitment to people and a style of life that was fascinating, intriguing, and magnetic. The words of his inaugural address in 1961 have already found a niche in American literature. Accepting the responsibility of government for a new generation and receiving the torch of freedom in their behalf, he described that generation in memorable phrases as "tempered by war and disciplined by a cold and bitter peace." Indeed, the people of the world gave their hearts to this American president with whom they could identify.

There is an Old Testament prophet who laid claim to the religious imagination. He is known only as Isaiah of the Exile and he lived and wrote during the period of the Babylonian captivity. His writings are to be dated about 540 B.C., a short time before the termination of the captivity. As a herald of God's eternal purpose he seized the imagination and hope of his fellow exiles and held their minds and hearts with the unrelenting tenacity of a prophet who knew his role and who was determined to hold them until they knew that role also.

Knowledge of the historical frame of reference for Isaiah's work and ministry is helpful if we are to gain meaningful insight into his writings. The Hebrews were still living with the bitter heritage of captivity. Since the destruction of Jerusalem they had carried an unforgetable burden of anguish. The last time they saw Jerusalem, its streets were crimson with blood, the Temple a rubbish heap. At the same time they had settled down into life in Babylon for the most part quite satisfactorily. Paul Scherer describes the situation in graphic language.

Upon large groups of these captive people the commercial spirit of the city laid fast hold, a hold that never has been relaxed! Some of them once again fell easily into idolatry. Others, more devout, kept alive the nobler elements of their ancient religion. They set for themselves certain intervals wherein to inquire of the Lord. They observed the Sabbath, and instituted four yearly feasts to commemorate the dark days of Jerusalem. Among them can be traced the first faint beginnings of the synagogue. But most significant of all perhaps was the renewed zeal with which they gathered their sacred writings for study. It has been suggested that much of the history of the Old Testament was during these desolate years arranged and edited, together with the prophetic literature and many psalms; perhaps even some codification of the law. To what extent this took place is uncertain; that under the influence of the Babylonian scribes and the great libraries of the city it was considerable, there seems no reason to doubt. One thing *is* certain: that when our unknown prophet of the exile enters on his mission he addresses himself to the remnant of a nation that for fifty years has been poring over the written Word of God and is tense now with expectation, looking for the Word's fulfillment.[2]

The tempo of the times quickened with the appearance of Cyrus on the horizon. Cyrus's rise to power was nothing short of meteoric. He made himself monarch of most of Asia Minor in a brief decade, took Babylon in 539 B.C. and made it and all its captive peoples vassals of his Persian Empire. At this juncture in history Isaiah of the Exile makes his impact on the exiles.

Paterson uses this historical event, the fall of Babylon, to date the writing of Isaiah of the Exile. "Cyrus had already entered upon his victorious career when the prophet began his work. Terror was already upon the peoples, and his rise had forced the powers to make a coalition against him. Croesus had sought support from Babylon, Sparta, and Egypt, but such alliances did not avail against the conqueror. Babylon had not yet fallen nor was Cyrus' edict yet published; thus we may date the prophecy between 549 and 539 B.C."[3]

I. A Message of Comfort and Hope

Isaiah of the Exile opens his message with words of comfort, hope, and consolation.

> Comfort, comfort my people,
> says your God.

---

2. Paul Scherer, *Event In Eternity* (New York: Harper and Brothers, 1945), p. 23.

3. John Paterson, *The Goodly Fellowship of the Prophets* (New York: Scribner's, 1950), p. 193.

Speak tenderly to Jerusalem,
 and cry to her
that her warfare is ended,
 that her iniquity is pardoned,
that she has received from the Lord's hand
 double for all her sins.[4]

Without the influence of Ezekiel and Isaiah of the Exile,
the Hebrews might have been totally absorbed by the imperial splendor of Babylon's culture. "In such a situation the
prophet is called upon to overcome those deadening doubts
and inspire the hearts of men with a mighty creative faith.
It is worthy of note here that the prophet almost uses the
word 'faith' but emphasizes rather the courage and resolution
that are the outward attitudes and expression of faith. 'Fear
not' and 'Wait' are his favorite words, and by these terms the
prophet signifies the militant aspect of faith, the capacity to
stand up to things and the ability to hold on to the very end.
For the prophet is bringing glad tidings of great joy. He comes
at a time when Israel was ground down to the dust. . . ." [5] In
such a time of overwhelming despair Isaiah is quick to promise comfort, hope, and consolation which are to be found in
a serene spirit. He promises redemption—a redemption that
shall manifest itself in an inward renewal of a personal spiritual life as God "blots out their transgressions."

But God's redemption of Israel has a social dimension and
perspective. Yes, God's eternal purpose envisions a new age of
release for the nation. It would be a new day of another
"deliverance from bondage," when the holy city would be
rebuilt to become a dwelling place for God.

When Isaiah of the Exile makes an emphasis on the social
side of their deliverance, this should remind us that the true
role of a biblical, prophetic religion is to bear witness to God's
graciousness in the totality of life. A one-sided adherence to
the personal aspect of the gospel in this day has caused the
church to skirt the crying issues of our generation. The

---

4. Isaiah 40:1–2, rsv.
5. Paterson, *op. cit.*, p. 195.

church has deserted its role as servant in the asphalt jungles of the inner city. Because of the wholesale acceptance of such a perversion of the gospel by the church itself, the pulpit squeaks out its innocuous words of good cheer and leaves the world to its crises and pains. The minister himself has swallowed the poison of such a viewpoint and deals only with vague, pious, sentimental generalities about "peace of mind" and "peace of soul." Pierre Berton indicts the Church in these words:

> In the great issues of our time, the voice of the Church, when it has been heard at all, has been weak, tardy, equivocal and irrelevant. In the basic conflicts that ought to be tormenting the Christian conscience, questions of war and peace, of racial brotherhood, of justice versus revenge, the Church has trailed.[6]

So, when Isaiah's message of comfort, hope and consolation involves the social dimension of God's redemption, I find a chastening word for the church that has failed to manifest concern for the dispossessed of the world. And there is no safe retreat for the church. The world of social involvement is a world wherein the church will be forced to champion some issues which will cost her members and financial support. But as far as I am concerned I had rather risk such costs than to be dismissed as unconcerned and irrelevant. You see, I am certain that the social dimension of the gospel lays its demanding claim on every man who takes seriously the teachings of the New Testament. And if the church heeds this word of Isaiah then it had better get involved where the real action is!

Life's ills and accidents have a way of draining the color and romance and vitality from our days. During days of tragedy we are inclined to forget the adventuresome quality of living. This was true for the exiles in Babylon, and Isaiah sought to buoy up their sagging spirits with his word of comfort and hope. "For while Cyrus was making history the prophet interpreted it in the light of divine purpose and

---

6. Pierre Berton, *The Comfortable Pew* (Philadelphia: Lippincott, 1965), p. 16.

showed the real significance of those momentous happenings. Behind all the international politics of his time he sees, and shows, the unfolding of Jehovah's purpose. And this he does to comfort hearts that were trembling and souls that were fainting amid the convulsions of that time." [7] So Isaiah pilots the exiles across the chasm of a thousand contradictions to the promise of God's presence.

II. A Message of Redemption and Deliverance

When we say that the unfolding of God's eternal purpose opens up life to the balm of hope and comfort, we are saying that God's divine purpose is redemption. Redemption is a necessity rooted in the very fabric of the created order. [8] Isaiah sees the exile as God's steady judgment against man's self-willed attempts to break away from him. But judgment is not the last word.

The history of Israel is a salvation history wherein God moves for the sake of all mankind. In Israel God has taken the initiative, working through the covenantal relationship established with Abraham—working in particular situations, in individuals, actualizing his grace in the arena of man's agony. The seeming chaos of history has a divine force at work in it! Scherer says,

> Someone outside the world had begun to speak. Leaning there against the throne of God he had caught with his quick ear the first faint, new stirring of mercy from those great lips. [9]

It was Isaiah of the Exile whose keen perception, sharpened by his vision of the glory and majesty of God, enabled him to see God at work in the throes of exile. He was at work to redeem, and

> back of the heathen temples, back of the rivers and the burning sun, back of the tramp of armies, along the winds of heaven, the messengers of Jehovah in their swift flight called out as they

---

7. Paterson, *op. cit.*, p. 195.
8. Scherer, *op. cit.*, pp. 105–106.
9. Scherer, *op. cit.*, p. 107.

passed, one celestial workman to another. God was set not on ruin but on rescue.[10]

As far as the exiles could determine, God was not visible on the rim of their captivity. The farthest edge of the horizon was dark, but Isaiah was a man of such sensitive sight that the faintest glimmer did not escape unnoticed. He was able to understand that God's divine purpose in history is redemption and that Israel was inescapably wrapped up in that purpose.

III. The Heavy Mantle of a "Servant" People

The vision of the prophet opened vistas of understanding concerning the destiny of Israel. Israel's task is set forth in the "servant songs." And here we run into problems. It is difficult to know whether the servant is the nation Israel, whether he is an individual, or whether the idea is to be referred to the messianic hope of Israel.[11] It seems to me that Isaiah sees the Servant as a small remnant of faithful Hebrews. He also views the remnant corporately as a person. But basically the nation of Israel is the Servant.

And, in this modern era, the church has fallen heir to the role of the Servant. In spite of its indifference, insensitivity, and unconcern, the church will truly be the church only as it becomes the servant of all mankind. The idea of a "smorgasbord" church must be hastened to an early death.

A "smorgasbord" church is a place where the personal and family needs of the members, the consumers, are primary. The consumer comes to buy what wares catch his fancy. The wares are displayed in the most attractive of Madison Avenue packages. It is the role of the layman to persuade the prospective buyer to come to market. Then the minister must persuade the prospective buyer to make his choice and purchase some of the available commodities— peace of mind, contentment, salvation.

---

10. *Ibid.*, p. 108.

11. The arguments concerning the various interpretations of "servant" can be found in any major commentary on Isaiah.

But this modern generation of sophisticates is not easily convinced. The salesman's pitch—even when packaged in new revivalistic forms—meets stronger resistance with each passing Sunday. Whatever can be prepackaged in a church—whether it be morality, middle-class suburban values, or patriotism in Christian guise—elicits little interest from this prospective buyer.

If the Church stands by this kind of a view, then its major concerns are related to preserving and enlarging the institution. In this view the *totality* of the church's ministry is related to preaching, the administration of the sacraments, education and recreational programs for children and youth, the winning of the nonchurched to church membership, the pastoral care of those caught in the throes of crises.

On the other hand, the understanding of the church as "servant" means that the church has a mission to society as well. This is not to deny the place and the function of the personal ministry. It is to say, however, that the church has a mission to the world and must give some priority to such matters as peacemaking and peace-keeping, the elimination of discrimination in employment and housing, the elimination of poverty. The gifted churchman Eugene Carson Blake put it like this.

> The Church must identify itself much more radically with the interest of the poor, the "losers," the outcasts, and the alienated. While one of the American Church's great strengths is its direct channel to the power structure of the nation through its most influential members, it will be disastrous if the Church pulls back from the course tentatively begun . . . in order to preserve undiminished this influence on the power structure. The mark of the presence of the awaited Messiah is still related to the poor having the gospel preached to them and the captives being released. The American Church would be foolish to ignore suburbia and the concerns of the influential members, but its life will depend on involving many of these members in the social revolution that will continue to develop in the cities of this nation.[12]

12. Eugene Carson Blake, *The Church in the Next Decade* (New York: Macmillan, 1966) p. 150.

The mission of the "servant" church, then, is to the whole world in travail and agony and pain.

This will be a costly and demanding task. But all the creative energy of God can flow into the church to empower it for the long pull of the task. It is nothing short of preposterous that the church has set the power of the gospel to the doing of such midget tasks. Paul Scherer puts it in these jarring words.

> We have to quit setting our faith such meager tasks and being content with such meager harvests! We dare not harness the tides of the Infinite to turn with them no more than a flutterwheel. We dare not garner the driving energies of this whole Creation, energies that hold the stars in space, that push up out of the hard earth the green of the spring like an army with banners: garner them one by one, to use them for no other purpose than to keep a civil tongue in our head! Heaven has not turned itself wrong-side-out for us to no end, running all its treasures on the sand for nothing! We make the religion of Jesus Christ ridiculous when we stoop with God in our hands to clear some silly things out of our way and are unable to heft it an inch! Get stuck in it ourselves. Or something somebody said once or did once keeps standing in the road grinning at us and making lewd gestures, holding us there cowed! This faith that subdued kingdoms, and stopped the mouths of lions, and quenched the violence of fire—come to that! Who wants it, if we can never *make* anything out of life with it? [13]

So I am not talking about an impossibility; I am talking about fulfilling a role that is the eternal purpose of God for his church.

Granted, the role of a "servant" church is a difficult role to fulfill. Such a role calls for measured discipline, for careful and imaginative strategies, and for the kind of sustained patience that will permit new serving structures to be created. This is not primarily a question of personnel and staffing, but of bold experimentation arising from determined commitment.

---

13. Scherer, *op. cit.*, pp. 220–221.

If the church is to reclaim its mission as "servant," it must be prepared to confess its sin in perpetuating inflexible structures that imprison men in physical, social, and mental ghettos. The church must confess its participation in the complicity of evils that plague men. Then a repentant church will be prepared to involve itself willingly in the secular orders of the common life. The church must identify itself with whatever there is of divine activity in politics, in community action organizations, in the labor-management realm, in commerce and industry, in the life of leisure. The church must sacrifice whatever prestige it has gained from being an accepted part of the Establishment in suburbia in order to identify with the socially and economically deprived of the city. The church must be ready to raise a red flag against the kind of inhuman warfare that we are waging in Vietnam, even if the cost is the loss of influence on the power structure. The church must seek to stop the brand of warmongering that has been able to justify war because of the economic reasons for such expenditures. The church must be a Good Samaritan to every pilgrim who has been beaten down by life's silent agonies between his Jerusalem and his Jericho.

Before that dream of a new age can come to pass, the church, the corporate community of God's people, must bear the heavy mantle of a "servant." It is called of God to the role of suffering and sacrificial service on behalf of all men. As the steward of God's eternal purpose in human history, the church must accept the demands and constraints such a stewardship lays upon it.

13. HAGGAI

On Preserving the Kernel

Scripture: Haggai 2:3–9

Gouverneur Morris was the United States Ambassador to the French Court of Louis XVI during the presidential administration of George Washington. He wrote to President Washington, "Louis XVI is a good man. In another generation he would have made a good king. The trouble is that he has inherited a revolution."

The twentieth-century church finds itself in the same position. It has inherited a revolution. And this revolution has eroded every facet of our common life. Our social life has become what Johnny Carson called an "orgy-catered" binge with self-gratification as its guideline. Integrity in public office has often been sacrificed on the altar of political expediency and popular appeal. The George Wallaces, more content with self-aggrandizement than with a selfless service of the public, clamor for a fragmented United States of America with a call to the states to abandon their national commitments and responsibilities for an aloof and selfish and closed state life. Domestically, many politicians are trying to force the poverty-stricken to beg, while proclaiming vociferously and hypocritically our national concern for the deprived.

We point to the lady in the New York harbor, the Statue of Liberty, as our symbol of openness. In her invitation

Give me your tired, your poor,
Your huddled masses, yearning to breathe free,
The wretched refuse of your teeming shore
Send these, the homeless, the tempest-tossed, to me:
I lift my lamp beside the golden door,

we proclaim our openness to receive all; yet there is discrimination in the total fabric of American life. We make
bold claims for our American experiment as the best example
of freedom for all. And yet we keep millions of Negro and
other minority groups of America economically imprisoned
on ante-bellum southern plantations, in urban ghettos and in
segregated hovels. Our historic national tradition and heritage of sympathy for the dispossessed has been ignored and
rationalized in the interest of our national security. Our post–
World War II commitment to an evolving organization of
enough international stature to arbitrate disputes in the
world community has never matured to its promise. We have
alternately viewed the United Nations as man's contemporary hope and as a foreboding threat to our hemispheric Mon-
roe Doctrine. We have conducted our international spying
with the deceit of the U-2 incident and the *Pueblo* incident
and with the immaturity of an emerging nation. This is a
description of a nation that has "inherited a revolution."

How has the church acted in these frightening years? Until recently when the "restless young Turks" began to rear
their heads and speak their minds, we have kept primly and
sedately silent. The church has acted like that "right harmless laddie" the old Scottish lady suggested was obviously
fitted for the ministry. Our Christian conscience has abdi-
cated its responsibility in the realm of controversial issues.[1]
Under the guise of being "in" the world but not "of" the
world we have drawn our robes of self-righteousness and
smugness around us and abandoned our servant role.[2] Instead of losing our lives in serving the world we have vaunted

1. Harry Blamires, *The Christian Mind* (New York: Seabury Press, 1963),
pp. 25 ff.
2. Alden D. Kelley, *The People of God* (New York: Seabury Press, 1962),
pp. 35–39.

an ecclesiastical and institutional expansionism. By so doing the church has abandoned the structures of the common life and has grown strong at the risk of its own life.[3] Thus, the principle of "death in order to live a resurrected life" is foreign to us. Hardened categories of institutional life and an impervious understanding of what is involved in being on mission to the world have been substituted for the primitive church's flexibility to change in the social order. A solidified dedication to a puritanical and Victorian prudishness in morality has taken the place of openness to the moral constraints which Christ ever lays afresh on the conscience of every sensitive Christian. As Koestler has his character Ivanov say in *Darkness At Noon,* "We are tearing the old skin off mankind and giving it a new one," and it is the business of the church to be vitally alive to what is happening!

If the new breed of clergy has anything to say about it, the church is going to speak relevantly to these issues. An article entitled "Revolt in the Church," by Harvard Divinity School Professor Harvey Cox, surveys the gathering storm that is seeking to drag the church, kicking and screaming, from its cloisters into the agony of life in the twentieth century.[4] The theologians are going to see to it that the church is aware of the inherited revolution!

In this kind of a revolution, just what is the place of the organized, institutional church in our society, if there is a place at all?[5] If, as it seems to me, the church is living out its life through heretical structures, if it is disobedient to the demand of the New Testament that it be a "servant" church, if radical reorientation is the only path to the renewal of the church,[6] we must conclude that the church as it is presently

3. Gordon Cosby, "Renewal in the Local Church," *Religious Herald,* February 4, 1965, p. 6.

4. Harvey Cox, "Revolt in the Church," *Playboy,* January, 1967, pp. 129 ff.

5. The more radical critics say that the church is already done in; see J. A. T. Robinson's *The New Reformation* (Philadelphia: Westminster, 1965), pp. 9–33 for these.

6. For an interesting proposal at this point see Stephen C. Rose's *The Grass Roots Church: A Manifesto for Protestant Renewal* (New York: Holt, Rinehart, Winston, 1967). Its thesis was first published in *Christianity and Crisis,* vol. 26, no. 13, July 25, 1966, pp. 168–71.

structured is denying the essence of its being, which is to die in order to bring resurrection life. What, then, is the church to do? The leader of an Evangelical Academy in Germany puts it graphically: "In folk dances in our country we talk about the 'standing leg and the playing leg.' " (The standing leg is the leg which bears the weight of the dancer; the playing leg is the leg that he uses to make figures in the air.) "The standing leg of the church at present is within the church and the playing leg is in the world. Somehow we have to reverse it. The standing leg must be positionized in the world and the playing leg must be in the church." [7]

At this point, the burden of Haggai is relevant and meaningful. His message is concerned with the survival and preservation of the people of God, with preserving "the precious kernel of Israel's faith," [8] that out of it may emerge a faithful people equipped to be servants of God's gracious, redemptive love.

Haggai's message is marked with the Hebrew genius for overwhelming intensity of purpose. His purpose is the rebuilding of the Temple. Cyrus's edict had permitted the return of the exiles to Palestine. There they had started to rebuild the Temple, but the work had lagged, and they needed the impetus of a passionate nationalist to keep them at their task. Haggai's writings are to be dated from September to December of 520 B.C. He is concerned with the institutional forms of Hebrew worship. He summons the people of Israel to a great corporate effort that will enable them to forget the past, and will give meaning and purpose to their individual lives and to their national existence.

I. Taking Seriously the Institutional Church

Many people in our day despise the institutional trappings of religion. But the word from the Lord through Haggai reminds us that institutional forms of religion must be taken seriously. So-called "religionless Christianity" fails right here.

---

7. Quoted in Cosby, op. cit., p. 6.
8. John Paterson, *The Goodly Fellowship of the Prophets* (New York: Scribner's, 1950), p. 226.

It is so severe in its condemnation of the institutional church that it becomes blind to the precious kernel of graciousness in the Christian faith.

"Religionless Christianity" is the contention that Christianity may exist independently of the organized church. It asserts that religion can become faith's worst enemy, that the church has become so absorbed in its housekeeping chores, so inflated by its status in society, and so lost in its ecclesiastical machinery, that the things that really matter most are neglected. The church has so insulated itself from the real issues, and from the things that matter most, that its concern for personal and social righteousness has been lost in the shuffle. It has cut itself off from the world's pain and agony.

Few critics maintain that all is well with the church. They are right in calling for renewal, for the restructuring of the church, and for Christian unity. Harsh and sobering criticism is not without its fruit. The criticism has served to shake the church from its apathy in many places. It has forced the church to desert its introverted and introspective concern of the past decade to move in mission to the world.

We need to remember, however, that it is well-nigh impossible to serve as a catalyst in a society adrift from its moral moorings, to serve as a rallying point for justice in the social order, to chasten the conscience of a nation hellbent on its destruction and that of all humanity with Vietnam as the scene of its demise, if there is no institutional structure to nourish and sustain the needs of the common life and to provide some visible sign of God's presence and continuing creative grace among men. It is an ephemeral idealism to think that Christianity is possible without some institutional forms and structures. Disembodied faith withers when it has no place to sink its roots for nourishment. Or, to change the metaphor, unfurling a banner is folly unless there is a staff from which it can flutter.

II. A Creative Place to Take Hold

Again, Haggai's word to us is that the Christian needs some place to take hold. Robert J. McCracken of the Riverside Church in New York City says that this is "the most important and perhaps least recognized need of the human soul." In reality, part of the turmoil in our cities is related to this need. Instability and rootlessness are conditions under which people live today. Their existence is brittle because they are not rooted in the rich soil of belonging.

Most of us have difficulty in finding a place to take hold because our God is too small. That is, our understanding of God is too immature for our understanding of the raw realities of life. J. B. Phillips, in his book entitled *Your God Is Too Small,* asserted that we need a remarkably enlarged understanding of God for this expanding universe. If we affirm every advance and every discovery as indicative of the magnitude of God's graciousness, then we will have some place to take hold. If we keep ourselves open to God and open to one another, then we can seek new insights into the constraints and demands that Christ ever lays on us afresh.

Modern life has been divested of its trappings and formalities and has been left bare and devoid of meaning. The play "Who's Afraid of Virginia Woolf?" is a commentary on the futility that is so characteristic of our day. But the play concentrates on a mood of meaninglessness and offers no way out of the morass of modern life, no way off the treadmill, no place for modern man to take hold. That is why I am afraid of Virginia Woolf—the play concludes that life is totally barren and sterile.

I am not suggesting that the ultimate seriousness of Haggai's word is that one must make his commitment to the institutional church in order to discover meaning. Rather, I am saying that modern man must take stock of his values, assess the things in life that matter most, and make his decision about the nature and quality of his commitments. It is only then that he can find some place to take hold. Once such decisions about his abiding commitments have been made, he must find some structures of the common life through which he can work and turn his commitments into active and meaningful reality. Starting with one's commitment to the institutional church is starting at the wrong end.

Bishop Robinson of Woolwich makes a strong case for this point in his book *The New Reformation*. In the chapter "Starting from the Other End," he contends that man's questionings begin with nature and not history. Man's quest for meaning begins with the quest for a gracious neighbor rather than for a gracious God. In other words, one must discover meaning in life *before* he can make a meaningful commitment to any institutional structure. One is first discovered by Christ and in the encounter meaning grips him. Then he seeks for some structured institution through which he can give active witness to that meaning. If the church will faithfully proclaim this quality of message to which a man may give commitment—the true gospel—then the institution need not fear. And even those who believe in the church will feel free to experiment with its construction, they will always want some kind of structure through which they can express their values.

III. Impossibility of Life Without Hope

Haggai has another heartening word for this day which has inherited a revolution—that no generation can live without hope. For his own day the prophet found hope in the person of Zerubbabel. Perhaps he was too quick at this point, but the message is clear. If we are to find purpose and meaning in life, then we must have hope about life.

The church must always hold out hope to every despairing man. Life for millions is a drab, anemic, colorless, and adventureless existence. The society in which modern man lives is frightening. The population explosion, the expanding industrialization, the continuing urbanization, the change in the social order, the depersonalization of life, the secularization of culture—all these give us reason for despair. It is at this precise point that Haggai becomes a live word of God for us. Haggai

. . . brings us far nearer to total truth of the Bible than once it did. The Bible is the record of God's acts of creation and redemption. In other days we felt ourselves challenged to try to share with God in his still unfinished creation of the world. The

ideal of a "creative life" was held before us as a valid interpretation of our religion. "Creativity" was to be a major virtue. But
today, and because of stern necessity, we are far more concerned
with the reconstruction of our world than with its further creation. To this extent the prophecy of Haggai takes its proper place
in a fully biblical view of life, for the Bible, after its serene beginnings, has much to say of the reconstruction of the shattered
fabric of society, and even more to say of the redemption of man
himself.[9]

The promise of such a possibility is the message of Haggai.

If the gospel has any crucial meaning for our day, in its
simplest terms it is that no man need remain the way he is.
Again and again in Christian history men have come to
grips with this fact and have started down a different road.
Life *is* reversible. This is not a static, inflexible world, and we
are not static individuals. Our world is throbbing and pulsating with life; it is pliable and dynamic. Ours is a world in
change, as James H. Laird put it in a sermon to his Central
Methodist congregation of Detroit, Michigan. He said, "Ours
is a world in process, a nation in process, a church in process
and we are individuals in process. There lies our hope that
the God who made us has not yet despaired of us and still
labors with us and for us to bring about his purposes."

Roman mythology has it that Jupiter sent Pandora, "the
gift of all the gods," down to earth. She was given a box but
was forbidden to open it. But her curiosity gained the upper
hand and she lifted the cover of the box and looked in. Immediately, every conceivable plague and evil escaped from
the box and were scattered throughout the entire earth. Pandora quickly shut the lid, but it was too late. Only one thing
was left—hope. Life without hope is meaningless. And
Haggai, as George Adam Smith put it, passed on to future
ages "an undiminished hope."

---

9. George A. Buttrick, ed., *The Interpreter's Bible* (New York: Abingdon,
1956), vol. 6, pp. 1042–44.

14. ZECHARIAH

Openness to Life's Pain

Scripture: Zechariah 2:4–11

In my estimation one of the most radical documents of our
American heritage is largely unknown. But its obscurity has
in no way diminished its impact on thousands of people
along the border of the United States and Canada. It began
as a proposal between the British and American governments
following the War of 1812. It was negotiated by Richard
Rush of the United States and by Charles Bagot of England
and, therefore, is known as the Rush–Bagot Agreement.

Following the War of 1812 the border between the United
States and Canada was heavily fortified. American and
British fleets patrolled the Great Lakes and eyed one another
with suspicion. On both sides of the border an armament
race appeared to be in the making. At this point Rush met
with Sir Charles Bagot and an original and daring policy
was set forth. The fortifications along the border were abandoned and the fleets were dismantled.

As one would expect, the agreement has led at times to
some hazards and to some uneasy intervals. Liabilities from
the viewpoint of the United States include those Canadian
citizens who work in the United States and pay little tax for
those services of government which make their employment
and travel more enjoyable. Furthermore, those who protest

the U.S. military conscription can travel freely to Canada, and remain there. From the viewpoint of the Canadians such an openness has placed heavy burden on the industrial life of Canada relative to a market for their products.

But when all of this has been said, the Rush–Bagot Agreement is illustrative of the fact that an openness between nations is not only possible but is beneficial to both. Border fortifications have been unnecessary and have become an anachronism. Fleets and patrols on the Great Lakes have been abandoned. This agreement, which is the first known instance of the limitation of armaments by international agreement, makes concrete the social view that openness is possible in the human community.

I. Accessible to All

The prophet Zechariah dreamed of the day in which Jerusalem would be a city open to the world, with a religious impact that flowed out to the ends of the earth so that everyone might have access to the city of God.[1] Zechariah was a priest who had returned with a group of the exiles from Babylon. His oracles are to be dated from November of 520 B.C. to December of 518 B.C. He was a contemporary of Haggai, although neither prophet refers to the other. One reason suggested for this is that Haggai may have been a member of the resident community at Jerusalem who escaped exile, and Zechariah a returned exile. The antipathy and hostility between those two groups is a fact of history. So, as if he were alone, Zechariah sets himself to his task with a passionate intensity— to inaugurate a new age of a new humanity proclaiming God's redeeming graciousness to the whole world that men might be made whole.

At the outset, we should note that Zechariah seeks to create a framework of understanding for his prophetic burden. Even though he is involved in the work of rebuilding Jerusalem, he asserts that the mechanics of worship are never to become

---

1. John Paterson, *The Goodly Fellowship of the Prophets* (New York: Scribner's, 1950), p. 232.

a substitute for obedience to the ethical demand of God. Zechariah seeks to make it abundantly clear that ceremony is never a proper end in itself. The vitality of worship is to be found in how well it equips the worshiper for his task in the common round of his existence. When worship and ceremony become a substitute for the very thing they are intended to enliven, then they become meaningless.

The situation which occasioned Zechariah's warning is found in Zechariah 7:1–7. In the midst of the task of rebuilding the Temple, a deputation from Bethel came to Jerusalem. Ostensibly, they came to ask about continuing the great fasts that had been instituted in the days of the exile. The spirit of the passage, however, suggests that the expressed purpose was not their real one. Bethel in Samaria was a rival shrine to Jerusalem; it is more feasible that their coming was related to their frequently expressed claim that Bethel was the one shrine for the correct worship of God. Zechariah seizes on this opportunity to blaze away indignantly at the kind of meticulous ceremony and ritual that neglects the weightier matters of justice and mercy. Any ceremony that neglects the true ends for which it was created is futile and courting disaster.

This is a relevant issue for any age. In many parts of the Christian church ritual has become a substitute for vital religious worship. Congregations have become a group of spectators gathered to watch the spectacle or drama that is going on in the chancel. Such worship does little in preparing the worshiper for that quality of life that he so desperately needs in this day of perpetual crisis.

What I long for in worship is a sense of excitement and adventure that comes from discovering the glorious freedom of the gospel. Worship must give us courage and serenity of faith to cope with life's pain and agony. Worship must convey acceptance and offer nourishment; it must provide the creative power through which one is propelled back into the world where he can be open to those who are gripped by the pain and struggle of life.

II. Military Defenses Unnecessary

Zechariah's dream of an open city, "as villages without walls," is a prophetic vision of peace for a war-weary world. In the ancient world a wall around a city existed for protection from the assaults of enemy troops. Zechariah longs for that time when such protection would be an unnecessary luxury. His vision in which this truth is cast is that of a surveyor laying down the limits for the walls of Jerusalem. But an angel bids another to inform the surveyor that God will be their rock, their fortress, and their might. In the coming new age, Zechariah is saying, there will be no need for walls, for the city of Jerusalem will be open to all the earth.

Walls shut out and exclude. Walls shut in and breed an inordinate sense of pride. Modern man needs to learn this truth. The Great Wall of China testifies to the fact that the survival of any civilization is not a matter of barricades. The steel and reinforced concrete of the Maginot Line bears its witness that no physical structure can promise peace. The Berlin Wall is a modern reminder that mortar and bricks are no barrier to the human spirit longing for freedom. And yet we refuse to learn the lesson of history. The bulk of our national budget still goes to defense and the frightening illusion that a "balance of terror" is the only way to keep the world free.

Furthermore, when one speaks of peacemaking and peacekeeping, the issue of our continuing presence in Vietnam comes to the fore. Our presence there raises serious questions about our claim to be a nation interested only in peace and in self-determination. The adminstration's recurring offer to "negotiate anywhere and anytime" sounds hollow against the background of dispute for peace talks and our predetermined conditions for negotiation. I long for that day when all America will be as "villages without walls," and yet I am alarmed by the fact that it looks as if there is not the flexibility of policy or the creative imagination in the administration to the extent that such a dream could be implemented on an international scale.

I cannot but view our policy in Vietnam as the fulfillment

of a commitment to a puppet government of our own creation, the justification of a bankrupt policy guided by a
military-defense-industrial establishment and the unimagi-
native expression of a pre-nuclear mentality bent on a military
victory. In my judgment, such a victory will, inadvertently,
deliver the moral leadership of the world into other hands
than our own. Furthermore, when General Westmoreland
spoke to the Congress in 1967, he made it abundantly clear
that we are building a military base in Vietnam in the event
it is needed against China. The proliferation of our mistaken
commitment to the military government can only be resolved
with a daring de-escalation of the conflict until such a time
the belligerents can meet in genuine negotiation. Then peace
can proceed meaningfully.

Zechariah had a glowing vision of Jerusalem in a new age
as a "village without walls" and this social view, exemplified
by the Rush–Bagot Agreement, has yet to be tried as an
option in international relations. I believe that America could
become a nation of such openness that she would be a source
of challenge and nourishment for the entire human community. I wonder if the church has the courage to set that
call ringing in the world? The Rev. Beverly Ashbury, preaching in Benton Chapel on the Vanderbilt University campus,
expressed it like this, "We cannot claim to be God-fearing
while being world-destructive. We cannot pretend to be ideal-
loving while overpowering small nations. The only way we
can hold our road together, bind up its wounds and make it
whole, lies in doing the truth, fulfilling our dream, our faith
in ourselves as a people." [2] May God help us to recover the
dauntless courage to become a nation so committed to peace
that we shall be open to life's pain.

III. Open to Life's Pain

So far I have suggested that it takes the vitality of worship
to sustain the person and nation open to life's pain, and that
such openness is a live option for a radical move in inter-

---

2. Quoted in the *Nashville Tennessean*, November 13, 1967, p. 9. Used with
permission.

national relations. Zechariah also envisions a new age wherein the people of God are fully and radically open to the suffering and pain of all men. The prophet had a burning hope that justice and freedom and meaning could be attained in a new age for a new Jerusalem. He dared to envision a world without disillusionment and discouragement. The rebuilding of the community was the first step in this direction, to create a structure for this new society. Thus, Zechariah committed himself to the task of reconstructing Jerusalem and of rebuilding the Temple. And this new Jerusalem would usher in a new age of a new peace.

If Zechariah were to be successful in realizing this dream, then a distinctive quality of life was essential. The visions of the flying scroll and of Madame Wickedness may seem bizarre but, essentially, they lay emphasis on the moral qualities which God has always demanded from his people. This had to precede the rebuilding of Jerusalem. Zechariah lays the demanding claim of God upon them, "These are the things that you shall do: Speak the truth to one another, render in your gates judgments that are true and make for peace, do not devise evil in your hearts against one another, and love no false oath." [3] No structure can ever survive without this sustaining moral quality.

In our day the renewal of society awaits for committed persons who have definite values. And here is where the witness of the church is so desperately essential. The people of God, whose commitment is to the value of persons, have a meaningful and live word of God for this day of crisis. The fragmentation of the common life is fact. The world is filled with people whose healing awaits the kind of acceptance and love that a person radically open to life's pain can give. These people need someone to reach out to them, to listen to them, to love them, to help them. They need someone to battle with them for urban renewal and housing and dignified employment and decent medical treatment. They need, as Ted Loder puts it, someone who "cares enough to keep pointing

---

3. Zechariah 8:16–17, RSV.

at the light and proclaiming there isn't enough darkness anywhere to put out one light." They need someone who "cares
enough to laugh and sing and rejoice in that wild assurance
that God's mercy does outrun our sin and his power does
overrule our impotence and that his purposes do undergird
our uncertainties."

But is the church a people of God who care that desperately? Is the church a people of God who are open to life's
pain? Is the church a people of God who are seeking to find
and support effective ways of alleviating human suffering, to
find relevant ways of ministering to people whose needs are
so complex? Is the church a people of God who care to reach
out to those who are groping in the dark despair of an unending night?

If we believe, as our Christian faith maintains, that people
are of supreme consequence, then let us seek out fresh ways
of guiding, nourishing, and sustaining them in this world of
pain and anguish. If we are true to our fundamental commitments, then we must quit locking ourselves off from the raw
realities of life. Zechariah had a dream of a new age wherein
the people of God are radically open to the pain of all men.

This openness to life's pain is dangerous. If one throws his
life totally open to all sorts and conditions of men, if one
seeks to accept the downtrodden and deprived of every segment of society, if one freely gives himself to others in life,
then he is opening his life to many dangers. People will
wound and hurt and abuse that person. By such action, the
person is becoming vulnerable to life's pain; he is becoming
vulnerable to whatever abuse people will push on him. C. S.
Lewis put it like this:

> To love at all is to be vulnerable. Love anything, and your heart
> will certainly be wrung and possibly be broken. If you want to
> make sure of keeping it intact, you must give your heart to no
> one, not even to an animal. Wrap it carefully round with hob-
> bies and little luxuries; avoid all entanglements; lock it up safe
> in the casket or coffin of your selfishness. But in that casket—safe,
> dark, motionless, airless—it will change. It will not be broken;
> it will become unbreakable, impenetrable, irredeemable.[4]

This quality of openness to life's pain, this compassionate concern for all people does make one vulnerable. It may mean that we are crucified by irredeemable hatred on twentieth-century gibbets. But only such openness of a people of God will permit the common community of humanity to catch sight of the turrets of the eternal city of God which is as a "village without walls."

---

4. C. S. Lewis, *The Four Loves* (New York: Harcourt, Brace and World, Inc., 1960), p. 169.

15. MALACHI

True Time's Advent

Scripture: Malachi 2:10–16

Reading the Bible seriously is a dangerous discipline! Too many people, however, assume the Bible to be a placid kind of book, even a little dull. It is too tranquil and drowsy to be interesting reading for modern folk. It is, this mood suggests, the very thing for a hot Sunday afternoon when folk take to nodding over their listless reading. But the real truth is that if people would read the Bible seriously they would discover that it is a dangerous book—with all the explosive power of a bomb. It has to be handled with extreme care if it is not to burst in upon our smugness with devastating consequences. Perhaps this is the very factor that contributes to making the world's best seller the least read book!

Furthermore, the Bible is to be taken seriously if its message is to become a live word from God. Written by men inspired by their understanding of God and his invasion of history, the Bible comes alive in every generation to those who take its message seriously enough to seek insight into its demand. Because its inspiration is rooted in an apprehension of God and of history, the Bible is as contemporary as the newspaper or the latest Broadway hit. It is relevant because it assumes the reality of man's need for meaning in any age.

Every generation is for some segment of the Bible what Browning termed "true time's advent" in *Paracelsus*.[1]

Because of time's erosion of our understanding of the historical framework that evoked a particular book, we may think that some segments of the Bible are no longer relevant to us. But just when we are on the verge of declaring a part of the Bible obsolete, history's changing cycles create an era in which that part becomes startingly relevant and meaningful. Particularly is this true of the burden of prophetic religion. This light which the prophets shed on this world come of age is astoundingly fresh and vital.

The sober return of our world to circumstances parallel to the day of the prophet Malachi has made his prophecy come alive to us even though on the surface the book appears arid and sterile. But with a little digging the challenge of its truth comes flashing through. Malachi rewards the sincere quest with the illumination of his prophetic insights. Today is "true time's advent" for Malachi.

In order to understand the relevancy of Malachi, we need to know how the historical circumstances of Malachi parallel the times in which we live. However, the precise historical situation in which God inspired Malachi is not plainly evident. The general nature of the period, however, and the diminishing quality of the national life can be seen in his prophetic message. Obviously, the exiles had had their souls scarred by the bitter frustrations of the era which followed their return to Jerusalem. They had looked forward to the end of the captivity with eager anticipation. The long journey they had seen as a pilgrimage to happiness, and the arrival at Jerusalem promised the renewal of their corporate life in a time of peace. The new age had promised to be a time for rediscovering and reclaiming their national integrity.

But the realities of those years proved that their fabulous dreams were well-nigh impossible. The barren and infertile lands made productive farming a galling and difficult task.

---

1. This emphasis was suggested by Willard L. Sperry in *The Interpreter's Bible* (New York: Abingdon, 1956), vol. 6, p. 1040.

So much energy was consumed by the drudgery of getting enough to live on that their dream of a new Jerusalem was a crushing burden. Indeed, "a spirit of dull depression settled over the community . . . and cynicism and impiety gained ground." [2] The high morale of the returned exiles was beginning to ebb.

When the Temple was finally completed in 516 B.C., a mood of despair and cynicism settled in on them, and for over a half century continued to be the prevailing spirit. In the midst of this apathy, Malachi was called to revive the flagging spirits of the returned exiles.

There are some obvious parallels between Malachi's age and our age. The fabulous dreams of the twentieth century have been difficult to bring to fruition. One world war was fought to make the world safe for democracy, and on the heels of that war another was fought to end all wars. The elusive dreams of peace have been shot through with the Korean "police action," the multiple Middle East crises, and Vietnam. I am convinced that so long as the economy of war-making gives such a large segment of our American society affluence, and so long as the economy of peacemaking and peace-keeping flirts with economic recession, then that long will the dream of peace be a flitting shadow. The conflict of realism with idealism has contributed much to an American mood of despair and frustration. Our attempts to build a meaningful society have been frustrated, with the result that cynicism and impiety have gained ground. This is why I am suggesting that Malachi is so relevant for the time in which we live.

I. Beyond the "Scandal of Particularity"

For one thing, our day is "true time's advent" for Malachi because he dared to look beyond the scandal of Judaism's particularity to the day wherein God would be worshiped as the God of the total human community. And this is a surpris-

---

2. George A. Buttrick, ed., *The Interpreter's Bible* (New York: Abingdon, 1956), vol. 6, p. 1118.

ing insight to be found in this prophetic burden. As Willard L. Sperry suggests in the *Interpreter's Bible*, such a brash and bold statement must have been regarded as "little short of treason and heresy."

At this juncture in the development of Israel, the recovery of the institutional structures of Judaism had been completed. But the ensuing tide of hope which rose to flood stage at the completion of the Temple had ebbed to a trickle. Zechariah's hope that Jerusalem would be an open city, open to the pain of the world, had not been fulfilled. His dream of Jerusalem's religious vitality flowing forth to the ends of the earth and of the earth's access to the city of God was still unfulfilled. The returned exiles who had lived through the agony of rebuilding Jerusalem and the Temple shared the disappointment that enfolded them when this dream finally died. And the Hebrews were unable to break this disappointment's lecherous hold on them.

As that tide of hope ebbed slowly away, their disappointment became despair, and their despair embittered them. Their neighbors treated them with a mocking disdain, unmindful of the fact that they construed themselves a chosen people through whom God would move to the world. The ebbing of their hope and the contemptuous attitudes of the neighboring tribes set them on edge. And it was but a short, easy step from there to derision of their relationship to God.

Parenthetically, it should be noted that this is precisely what happens so much of the time in the church today. Spirits which had been kept high by the fevered intensity of providing adequate building for worship and Christian education begin to sag when the work is done. Problems which are often forgotten, overlooked, or deferred because of the demanding claim and pressure of building can be magnified out of all proportion when the building is finished. The high tide of enthusiasm about building becomes the low ebb of ruptured relationships. The most innocent and innocuous of remarks can be redirected toward personal hostility. The energies which were directed toward a visible goal are redirected toward persons.

At this point Malachi broke the prophetic silence with his oracles. He addressed himself to those Hebrews whose despair and cynicism about their place in history had caused their worship of God to deteriorate. He denounced their personal insincerity in worship, as evidenced by the fact that they had neglected Temple worship. He denounced their flagrant personal immorality as evidenced by their fraud and adultery. He denounced their social sins as evidenced by the oppression of the poor and the perjury of justice. He denounced their folly in "dealing treacherously with their brothers." [3]

"You are totally blind and insensitive to the real character of the God whom you presume to serve," he told them. "If you will review our national history then you will find that God is abundant in mercy and extravagant in his graciousness. If you continue in your stubborn rebellion then God will place you under judgment and create a new order in which justice and righteousness shall prevail. There is a purpose of God running the entire fabric of history and in the end that purpose will be realized."

II. Humanity's Inherent Reverence for God

Malachi speaks of the fact that God is the creator of all mankind and is the God for whom the heathen nations have an inherent and native reverence. Isaiah of the Exile had given this concept its sublimest and most classic expression, and here the same exalted idea breaks through the illuminating spirit of the prophet Malachi.

The exiles had returned to Jerusalem with the high hope of launching a universal religion. But with the renewal of the structures of Israel's worship, this hope became introverted and particularistic. Malachi noted that the Hebrews were moving away from the implication of Jerusalem's being an open city, and announced that it was presumptuous folly to assume that God was concerned only with his people Israel. God is the creator and sustainer of the total human com-

---

3. Malachi 2:10, KJV.

munity. He cares for all men equally, and it is his will that we should live together in community.

This very truth is the bane of the church today insofar as the church has not acted to make brotherhood a reality. We proclaim that God is the God of all the nations and, yet, we refuse to accept every man as our brother. But the truth of the matter is that there is no way to deny brotherhood except as it is a denial of our sonship! The refusal to accept the Negro as a brother is, in reality, not a denial of our inherent relationship as brothers; rather, it is a denial of our common sonship under God the Father. Ultimately, we shall have to accept our brotherhood.

This truth is illustrated in a story by Thomas Carlyle. He tells of a stricken widow who appealed to her neighbors for help. They refused to help her on the grounds that what happened to her was no concern of theirs. The end of it all was that she died, but not before she had infected the entire neighborhood with typhus. Carlyle's comment was, "She proved her sisterhood. Her typhus fever killed them. They were brothers even though they denied it." It is my contention that there is no final way to deny our brotherhood. Such refusal to accept all people as our brothers is but a mocking denial of our created status under God.

Looking candidly at my own ministry as the pastor of a local congregation is a traumatic experience. I am quick to press the fact that I will not serve as the minister of a congregation which practices segregation. I contend for an open church and a free pulpit. But, in reality, my own ministry has degenerated to a practice of the same segregation that I condemn so piously from the pulpit. I have not made pastoral counseling and calling available to the black community as I have sought to do to the rest of the community in which I serve. In theory I have been swift to condemn the contention of the segregationist that there are master races with some permanently inferior and others permanently superior. But, in practice, I have refused to act on this basis. I have continued to perpetuate a type of ministry wherein color, social class, and economic factors dictate a church that is actually closed, at the same time proclaiming that the gospel is for all men. Basically, my actions deny my vaunted claim that I preach the whole gospel to the whole world that men may be whole. Repentance is in order for me more so than for the most radical of the segregationists.

I wonder if this is not the case with many of the men of the cloth who construe themselves "liberal" in the area of race relations! It is my intention to reverse my practice and to seek to make my ministry available to every person regardless of race, color, or creed. I could wish that this confession of my personal sins at this point might serve to chasten and challenge other ministers to reexamine the practice of their pastoral ministries.

The call, then, from Malachi is for the church in this present decade to throw its full weight into the struggle for justice. The church must support the efforts of all men of good will to eliminate the cancerous racism that is still so characteristic of much of American society. The church must get involved in opening the local congregation up to any person who comes to worship, regardless of his motives, his color or his station in life. The church must involve itself in the struggle for equal employment opportunities. The church must involve itself in demonstrating the reality of its proclamation that every man is brother. To do less is to deny our sonship!

III. Celebrating the Continuing Creativity of God

Again, this is the decade of Malachi's "true advent" because his prophetic message takes a high view of marriage. At this interval one finds another of those surprising insights that come surging out of the prophet's writing. And this is a needed and relevant word for a generation in which there is an obvious change in today's family patterns.

Many peddlers of gloom are quick to contend that the shifting moral emphasis of our day is markedly downward. But it is the contention of the most sensitive and gifted specialists that the impression of gross moral degeneration is false and misleading. Rather, the shift in emphasis and the change is a sign that the standards are going up. Professor Lynn White of UCLA says, "Morose pontification on the disintegrating and decay of society is based on a very limited selection among the facts of our time. The full view of the facts justifies not gloom but exhilaration." [4]

Just what was happening in the community that merited the censure of the prophet with reference to marriage is not clear. But Hebrew society was basically dominated by the men. The right of the husband to divorce his wife was seldom questioned. This assumed privilege was a source of much scandal in the society of the Hebrews. In later Judaism a man could put away his wife if she burned the biscuits or if he found a more beautiful woman. Malachi condemns this practice as fundamentally an abuse of persons.

Divorce and the disintegration of family life are major problems in the United States. There are some 400,000 divorces granted in the United States each year with about 300,000 children involved in these divorces. This situation has come about for many reasons. The revolutionary world situation has an unsettling effect that has made an easy hedonism possible. The population shifts to the cities have made anonymity more possible. The dehumanizing processes of automation and cybernation have taken a toll. The influence of the recreational view of sex as epitomized by Hugh Hefner's playboy empire has diluted and dissipated the impact that the Christian understanding of marriage has had on our culture.

We need to hear the word of the Lord through Malachi asserting that marriage is a covenant and commitment that is no less sacred than one's relationship to God. We need to understand that the marriage relationship can be a joyous celebration of the handiwork of God. We need to reject the counterfeit gospel that makes marriage and sexuality a concession to the flesh and recognize that marriage is meant to be the continuing communication of two authentic human

---

4. Lynn White, Jr., "On Intellectual Gloom," *The American Scholar,* Spring, 1966, p. 224.

beings. We need to reject the equally counterfeit gospel of the "playboy" view of sexuality as blissful when moral inhibitions are gone and when consent is present. We need to realize that marriage involves the matter of treating persons as persons, as Joseph Fletcher contends, with unconditional seriousness.

Melvin E. Wheatley of the Westwood Community Methodist Church of Los Angeles puts it this way:

> A part of the strong medicine of our Christian ethic of love is to stimulate within us . . . discontent with anything less than the . . . supreme meanings that are intended to be present in the physical relations of sexuality. The physical sexuality of which God approves is intended to be something infinitely more personal, more social, more permanent than the momentary titilation of a complex of highly sensitized nerve endings. It is meant to be the continuing communication of two authentic human beings saying to one another through their actions . . . I love you! It is when the physical expression of human sexuality is handled with that kind of sensitivity that it becomes an experience not only of which God heartily approves, but of which man proves he is capable of making—a miracle.[5]

So a confrontation with Malachi proves to be a rewarding study. He is under no illusions about either the degeneracy of its religion or the decay of public morality. And yet he insists that some institutional structures are necessary. Some would dismiss Malachi for this insistence. But to do so is to close a book from which surprising insights emerge. After all, this is the strange way God works. When we have our affairs neatly arranged and securely pigeonholed, God comes crashing through with some surprising revelation of himself. This is the way Malachi's message has its advent. From this small, seemingly insignificant book we learn that the total human community belongs to God, that all people have an inherent and native reverence for God, and that marriage is an avenue open for men and women to affirm and celebrate the continuing creativity of God.

---

5. From an unpublished sermon, "Man Cannot Live by Bed Alone," and used with permission.

16. JOEL

Man's Agony and God's Grace

Scripture: Joel 2:10–13

In the years 1348 to 1350 the whole of western Europe suffered the most widespread and deadly epidemic disease in its history. The Black Death, a form of the bubonic plague, reached into every city and village, its spread accelerated by merchant ships from the East. The population of Europe was decimated by a third.

The United States of America has known little or nothing about the sweeping devastation of national disaster. Since the majority of Americans are under 25 years of age, the experience with rationed staples of World War II is unknown to them. Even fewer remember the pains and deprivations of the Depression. And the national disaster of the Civil War haunts only a few dedicated historians. To most of us national disaster is not a reality.

The closest we have come to a disaster of national proportions in recent years has been the crisis of the cities. Because discriminatory employment practices, an inferior education system in the ghettos, and racial discrimination are inflammable materials, small incidents have ignited the ghettos with the fires of a seething discontent. The restless despair of the deprived peoples of the cities reached an epidemic stage in Los Angeles, Chicago, Newark, and Detroit. I do not believe them to be organized campaigns as some do; I see them as the spontaneous combustion of a neglected people. The riots are "the spasmodic explosions that occur when some random incident strikes the tightly packed dynamite of despair." [1]

But what disturbs me is the intransigent posture of many public officials. Police force is necessitated by the rioting, but one does *not* deal with the roots of our urban crisis by such action alone. The refusal to eliminate racial discrimination is simply delaying the inevitable explosion. The refusal to alter the shape of things in discriminatory employment practices, to improve urban ghettos, to deal with the pockets of poverty in the slum areas tends to deliver power into reckless hands—for instance the more irresponsible forms of Black Power. It pushes many ghetto-dwellers to the inescapable conclusion that only what *The Christian Century* calls "conspicuous irrationality" will provide the tool for the eradication of the social ills of the day. If this does become a tragic necessity, then all of us will taste the bitter fruits of a national disaster in the cities.

This brings us, then, to the book of Joel. Joel's prophetic utterances were given against the backdrop of national disaster. Joel is an elusive, receding personality as far as history has been able to discern. And the meaning of his oracle is only a little clearer than the image of himself he has left us in his book. The national disaster which called forth his words was the invasion of a horde of locusts. The date for his writing has been suggested by some scholars as the fourth century B.C. The terrible plague of locusts and the accompanying drought occupy his mind because he believed that such disaster was an index of divine displeasure.

I. An Occasion for National Repentance

The first truth that comes to us out of Joel's book is that the phenomenon of disaster should always be an occasion for

---

1. From an editorial, "Conspicuous Irrationality," in *The Christian Century*, August 2, 1967, p. 987.

national repentance. As far as Joel is concerned, the calamity and disaster of his day superceded anything that had ever happened in his experience. That plague of locusts had no precedent or parallel in Hebrew history. No one was able to escape its effects.

Joel views the locust plague as an index of the religious defection of Israel. There was moral disorder in the created world and the plague came as a call from God to bring men to repentance. Of course, man can respond to disaster in other ways. He can assume the stance of a stoic and simply endure the calamity. He can seek to be brave and courageous in the face of affliction. From Joel's viewpoint such action ignores the somber facts of human sin. The ruptured relationships between men, and between men and God, will not be restored by stoicism. Rather, life's renewal awaits a repentance that invades the inmost recesses of the springs of inner life. This is why Joel calls men to repentance.

Recent history is a meaningful parallel here. The assassinations of John Kennedy, Martin Luther King, and Robert Kennedy were disasters of national dimensions. Whether or not the nation responded with a corporate repentance to these killings, we were certainly encouraged to do so and to think over our possible national failure. This was the response Joel was seeking to elicit from Israel—a sense of sorrow for national wrong and failure, and a turning to God. Beyond the vicissitudes of history, beyond the ebb and flow of human fortune, beyond the disasters which sweep their relentless course across the world, God stands ready to enter into the depth of our need. The only way in which a person should react to any crisis of historical portent is with what Carlyle Marney terms "a proper sorrow"—sorrow appropriate to the occasion.

Our reaction to disaster is important because of our tendency to become rigid and inflexible. We search for a way of life in which we can feel secure, and try to settle down into some system or structure. The longer we are at home in such a structured existence, the more rigid and inflexible we become as persons. In that comfortable shell we become immune to people and their need of acceptance, forgiveness, and affirmation. So that when some disaster comes crashing through our closed system in which we are isolated from the raw realities of the world, we are forced to look into the depths of our being for sustaining power to bring us through the time of crisis. And we discover that there is none; our inner being has shriveled. Disasters drive us from our shells to the world of pain and travail. This is always a shattering experience—to find the springs of our inner nourishment arid and sterile. But only then can change come, only then can we make our response to God's offer of his graciousness.

II. A Stepping-Stone Rather Than a Stumbling-Block

Another emphasis that emerges from the prophetic utterances of Joel is the truth that the disasters and agonies of life can be stepping-stones rather than stumbling-blocks. Disaster has a dual potential. It contains within its harshness either seeds for decay or seeds for healthy growth. Disaster clamors on the one hand that we succumb to its deep anguish. But on the other hand, it is not in our nature to have things easy. Rather, it is our nature to achieve and fulfill. We demand challenge and adventure to grow. And that may involve disaster and agony.

Perhaps the story of Brian Sternberg will illumine this truth. As a sophomore at the University of Washington he broke the world's record in the pole vault. Some time later he was getting back into trim on a trampoline, lost his balance, fell, and suffered a spinal injury that left him paralyzed. Since that time he has demonstrated his championship qualities in the area of handling disaster. He was able to take a stumbling-block and turn it into a stepping-stone as far as the way he learned to handle life. One day one of his uncles visited him in the hospital and, trying to be helpful, said, "Brian, I wish I could take your place for a week and give you some rest." Brian replied, "You couldn't do it. I know because I couldn't either, if I didn't have to!"

If a person can face the disasters of his personal experience with that kind of courage, then he will find the resources that

are needed to meet the demands of tomorrow. Confidence is
not a means of escape; rather, it is a means of waging the
battle and coming through it victorious. The disasters of life
remind us that life is frail and fragile. And, somehow, we
must find the courage and strength to transform those
stumbling-blocks into stepping-stones which take us to maturity in life.

III. The Healing Balm of God's Generous Grace

Joel declares at the climax of his argument that the disaster
of the locusts is an index of Israel's defection. The only thing
that the people can do is to repent and prepare for the inevitable day of the Lord. And, yet, there is room for the judgment to be turned back. George Adam Smith puts it like
this:

> His Day is about to break. From this it is impossible to escape on
> the narrow path of disaster by which the prophet had led up to
> it. But beneath that path the prophet passes the ground of a
> broad truth, and on that truth, while judgment remains still as
> real, there is room for the people to turn from it. If experience
> has shown that God is in the present . . . faith remembers that
> He is there not willing for judgment, but with all His ancient
> feeling for Israel and His zeal to save her.[2]

So there is yet deliverance from God's judgment through repentance!

In conclusion, Joel describes God as extravagant in his
mercy and generous with his grace. Here is the way he
writes of God's grace. "Return to the Lord, your God, for he
is gracious and merciful, slow to anger, and abounding in
steadfast love."[3] There is a depth of insight that is characteristic of the New Testament. God gives himself without stint,
asking nothing in return.

The Bible does not content itself with the sordid story of
man's sin and agony. That theme is there, but it is not the

---

2. George Adam Smith, "The Book of the Twelve Prophets," *The Expositor's
Bible* (Grand Rapids: Eerdmans, 1947), vol. 4, p. 660.

3. Joel 2:13 rsv.

major one. The major theme of the Bible is God's grace. Joel moves beyond tragedy to the God of all history who proffers his grace. Behind the tragedy of our frail existence is God! And God is ready to deliver!

God is an extravagant God. Edmund Steimle reminds us that this is a characteristic of God we find hard to understand. We call prudence and caution very proper virtues and find it inexplicable that God should waste nature's lush extravagance on the tropics, and the unnecessary vastness of the universe on that which can't appreciate it.[4]

God is also extravagant with man, touching us with the incredible generosity of his love and grace. Viewing the way man has abused these gifts, we are uncomfortably aware that prudence would have been a less costly virtue for God. Because men were lost in meaninglessness and plunged in despair, God broke into the arena of life himself. He gave us himself in Jesus, bridging the gap between his grace and our need. God's extravagance was a person, living as all men live, being tempted as all men are. In Jesus a mirror is held up to the depths of every person. His presence seeks us to accept us and to affirm our potential and worth. In Jesus God keeps his tryst with all mankind, and in his extravagant graciousness is our hope.

Can twentieth-century America learn a lesson from disaster? Since Watts, a disaster of national proportions has been threatening America. It has taken the shape of the crisis of the cities. It is fed by the grossest inequities of our social structure—slum housing, inadequate education, discrimination in employment. Joel is a word of God for this crisis. He suggests that we transform the looming disaster into a stepping-stone rather than allow it to be a stumbling-block. It may very well be that God is prepared to use this crisis for our growth. The crisis could drive us out of our cloisters into the real world. There, breathing the fresh air of God's live word, we may be forced to recognize that God's

---

4. Edmund A. Steimle, *Are You Looking For God?* (Philadelphia: Fortress, Press, 1957), p. 147.

boisterous spirit can never be contained. And we may also be forced to accept the potential tragedy of this crisis in order to transform the cities of man's agony into refreshing centers where God's graciousness flows to the healing of man's hurt.

17. JONAH

An Indefatigable Love

Scripture: Jonah 3:1–4:2

If I were to dub the Old Testament book of Jonah with some other name I would be tempted to use Andrew Dickson White's verbose title, *A History of the Warfare of Science with Theology in Christendom*! It is a tragedy that for centuries controversy has obscured the central issue of this little book. And as the waggish tongues have it about one's mother-in-law, the battles which have raged around Jonah have overstayed their welcome. Even the most ardent protagonists are aware that the warfare has kept the impact of Jonah submerged. Yet, controversy still hangs on, thick as a London smog.

Nonetheless, it is the intention of this sermon to move beyond the arena of such jousting between science and religion to the more meaningful issues of this prophetic utterance. I want to avoid the border skirmishes so that we can wrestle with the major emphases of the book. And I shall seek to interpret Jonah as an Old Testament parable, similar to the New Testament parables of Jesus, that needs to be treated in a similar fashion. The central issues of Jonah have little to do with the matter of a fish swallowing a prophet; rather, the central thrust lies in the insight, as Robert J. Arnott put it, that "Jonah swallowed a whale." He believed that Israel's role as a "chosen people" was exclusive, and that was the "whale Jonah swallowed!"

162

The author of the book of Jonah was a man who was able to assert an inspired truth with imagination, precision, and genius. The book was probably written near the close of the fourth century B.C., in a time of fanatical nationalism in Judea.

During the Babylonian captivity, Isaiah of the Exile sought to move beyond the trauma and tragedy of captivity to a day of hope. He sought to buoy up the sagging spirits of the Jewish captives. The prophet looked beyond the farther rim of Israel's immediate horizon to see that God's divine purpose in history inescapably involved a "servant" nation in the redemptive purposes of his grace. Isaiah taught them to yearn for that day of deliverance and to long for the new age. The deliverance under Cyrus was understood to be the outworking of God's eternal purpose for his people. Therefore, when the exiles returned to Jerusalem in 538 B.C., their mood of celebration was not dissimilar to the mood of the exodus. They were returning with high hopes and lofty ideals, for they were to be an instrument for the initiation of a new age. But, before much time intervened, the vision and dream began to wither and die, shattered by the realities of the situation. There was strife and conflict between those who had remained in Jerusalem and Judea and those who were returning from Babylon. There was a succession of crop failures and of efforts to rebuild the Temple. All of this struggle sapped their energies and depressed their spirits.

It is easy to understand, then, how they succumbed to the temptation to structure a society in which they, God's chosen people, would be safe from their enemies. This outpost of exiles became more and more exclusive. The idea of a "servant" people was soon lost, and those nations Israel was supposed to serve became the objects of hate and invective. They had deserted the concept of God's universal love, and now "they looked forward to the day when God would exalt them and give vent to his wrath upon their neighbors and overlords. Judaism had become ingrown, with an emphasis upon legalism, ritual, and the priestly functions" [1]

---

1. J. Elliott Corbett, *The Prophets on Main Street* (Richmond: John Knox, 1966), p. 71.

At this precise point "an anonymous Jewish religious thinker wrote a parable to jolt his countrymen out of their provincialism, to rekindle the missionary zeal of Second Isaiah, to remind them they were chosen by God to be a light to the Gentiles." [2] And if we are to understand Jonah, to accept his insight, and to profit by this lively word of God, then we must pause to comprehend the nature of the vehicle which was chosen to convey the message of God.

Here is an effective way of presenting crucial truth—by means of a parable the message of Jonah reaches the heart as well as the head. It begins with a story wrapped around the historical figure of a prophet who lived during the reign of Jeroboam II. Jonah was a prophet with an unalterable strand of nationalism in his prophetic utterances. He was a prophet of the kind of Judaism which asserted the exclusive claim of Israel to God's graciousness and mercy. As the writer weaves his story around Jonah he "probes the conscience, stirs the emotions and challenges the minds" [3] of his readers. The Book of Jonah has the effect of throwing open the windows of Israel's soul so that the light of God's purpose might illumine their darkness and lack of understanding. The Book of Jonah has as its purpose to show that

> There's a wideness in God's mercy
> Like the wideness of the sea;
> There's a kindness in his justice,
> Which is more than liberty.
>
> But we make his love too narrow
> By false limits of our own;
> And we magnify his strictness,
> With a zeal he will not own.
> —FREDERICK W. FABER

The parable begins with God calling Jonah to fill a prophetic role and continues with God bidding him to go to Nineveh to announce judgment on the Assyrians. But Jonah

---

2. *Ibid.*
3. Harold A. Bosley, *He Spoke to Them in Parables* (New York: Harper, 1963), p. viii.

stubbornly refuses and asserts his rebellion by heading west to Tarshish. The calamity of a storm at sea and the episode with the fish ensue. Again the insistent call of God breaks through the clamor of Jonah's self-assertions, and this time Jonah heads for Nineveh to proclaim judgment and destruction. The only avenue for the salvation of Nineveh is repentance, and Nineveh responds on a national scale. Jonah reacts with bitter anger because God has chosen to show compassion and grace to these foreigners. Far from desiring their deliverance, Jonah had consoled himself and had justified his trip to Nineveh with the eager anticipation of the Assyrians' imminent destruction.

I. Man's Eternal Attempt to Escape God

Is there a quickening and living word of God for us in this story? Indeed there is. The first truth that breaks out of this parable is related to our own response to the love of God for the total human community. In Jonah's flight from God is to be found a vivid picture of man's eternal endeavor. Man, created to go God's way, has an inveterate tendency to take his trips to Tarshish. Man has always used every stratagem at his disposal to put distance between himself and God. He tries to elude God's demands on his life, to run away, to escape God by pretending not to hear his voice.

The story of Adam and Eve in Genesis is a pointed disclosure of man's primitive attempt. It is a transcript of every man's experience, trying to get away from God. The ancient record expresses it this way, "And the man and his wife hid themselves from the presence of the Lord God among the trees of the garden." Man puts himself and his will at the hub of his life. He deifies himself, turning away from his true God, furtively scurrying off to avoid encountering him.

Take the thesis of the "Fugitive," as it was unrelentingly pursued on television. Richard Kimball is a symbol of man, a fugitive and vagabond in flight from God.

The conclusion of the matter is, however, that no man can by flight escape God. Jonah learned this lesson from his experience. He fled to Joppa and boarded a vessel bound for

Tarshish. He paid his fare and carried his bags below. But, as he suspected all along, he couldn't get away from God's haunting presence. Every avenue of escape was a dead end. God's claim was laid on him a second time.

Finding this to be our experience, too, modern man seeks other ways to elude God. Unable to escape by flight he seeks to hide. Whenever we are confronted by the insistent clamor of his voice in the recesses of our lives, when the searing light of his goodness falls full on the darkness of our sins, we try to hide. There are many and devious ways of hiding, but none of them work. You may isolate yourself in some impregnable fortress, crowd your walls with sentries and surround yourself with countless alarms and defenses, but you are powerless to withstand God's onslaught. God is inescapable; you cannot hide from the searching scrutiny of his seeking. History reveals that God is forever breaking in on us in new and surprising ways and there is no way to hide.

Literature bears its witness to this universal experience of man. Francis Thompson strove to escape God and hide from him. But, he testifies that "The Hound of Heaven" kept his "strong Feet" ever in pursuit. Augustine's *Confessions* is the record of his running away from God and his attempts to hide from God. Yet, he concludes that every man is restless until he rests in God. Dostoevsky's *Crime and Punishment* concludes with the fact that finally God breaks in upon a man. God closes in upon us even while we are hiding, and there is no escape until we have dealt with him.

Evasion can become a sophisticated affair. Unable to run away and unable to hide we try to expel God from the common round of our existence. The history of Israel says that the people tried to confine God in the ark, enshrine him in the Holy of Holies, and blind his vision with the smoke of sacrifice and incense. And, today, we deport God to a towering cathedral, circumscribe him in a creed, or cage him in a musty, untouchable book. But God is too boisterous to be contained. He keeps battering down cathedral doors, breaking out of our creedal structures and snapping the bonds of our neatly wrapped books. He insists on intruding into places he is not invited. God always comes bounding back into life from the exile we have sought to impose upon him.

So the truth comes surging in upon us. There is no way to escape God or hide from him or evade him. Dr. Steimle puts it like this in his sermon "The Reluctant Prophet."

> He always does catch up with us sooner or later in some storm of life, whether it be a civilization, a nation or an individual like you or me. . . . Look at the nations. They too were going merrily about their business of exploiting the riches and cheap labor of Africa, India, China, and the exotic and fabulous lands and islands of the South Seas, until the storm came, and now whole continents are in revolt against white empires built on colonialism with its double standard of values for white and colored. The communist threat in those areas, dangerous as it may be, must not blind us to the deeper motivation behind this large-scale revolution on the part of the colored peoples of the world. God has caught up with us Christian white people in the storm over Asia and Africa. There is no escape from God. You know it and so do I. And so did Jonah! [4]

There is no way around God!

II. Common Humanity Revealed in Common Peril

Another quickening word of God slipped up behind Jonah. Even as he sought escape, the churning sea blocked his flight. Thinking the storm was a punishment for his rebellion, Jonah proposed to calm the raging elements by throwing himself overboard.

In the crisis of a storm at sea, threatening his life and the lives of all on board, new insight broke over him and engulfed him, if even only for a brief moment. The common peril reduced all on that ship to the level of their common humanity. Those pagan sailors refused to honor Jonah's suggestion, and rowed all the harder for the shore. Jonah's hatred for anything not Jewish was challenged in that struggle at sea. Their common peril had forced him to accept

---

4. Edmund A. Steimle, *Are You Looking For God?* (Philadelphia: Fortress 1957), pp. 86–87.

their common humanity and his prejudices were forgotten for that quick moment.

The story should serve to prick the conscience of the church. At the beginning of its life the church was a fellowship that transcended all social and racial barriers. They understood Jesus' word as emphatic and unambiguous. He spoke of God as the Father of all mankind whose paternity made all men brothers. He taught that there are no inferior races. The primitive church was a community of love in which this reality was lived out to the fullest. It brought together those who were alienated and estranged. The common bond of their allegiance to Jesus Christ brought together rich and poor, slave and free, educated and uneducated, laborer and capitalist. In this day of racism, rampant and radical, the church must relearn this lesson of its heritage.

Jonah's prejudice was thrown into such a crisis that he offered to throw himself overboard to insure the survival of the ship. Obviously, from the story's indication of other struggles with his prejudice and hatred as he sat overlooking Nineveh awaiting its destruction, we must not make too much of the action. But it is poignantly symbolic. If ever the racial prejudice of our day is to be totally eliminated the church must be willing to throw itself into the struggle, "to throw itself overboard."

The Christian church has a poor record at this level. National conventions and assemblies have condemned racial wrongs at every recent meeting. At the same time, the church has been extremely cautious and sinfully reticent in exerting concrete influence. With the exception of individual Christians the church is guilty of neglecting to act concertedly to eliminate racism. This reticence on the part of the church and the clergy was in for a scathing indictment in that modern epistle of Martin Luther King entitled "Letter from Birmingham Jail." He wrote,

> In deep disappointment I have wept over the laxity of the church. . . . So often the contemporary church is a weak, ineffectual voice with an uncertain sound. So often it is an arch-defender of the status quo. Far from being disturbed by the

presence of the church, the power structure of the average community is consoled by the church's silent—and often even vocal—sanction of things as they are. But the judgment of God is upon the church as never before. If today's church does not recapture the sacrificial spirit of the early church, it will lose its authenticity, forfeit the loyalty of millions, and be dismissed as an irrelevant social club with no meaning for the 20th century. Every day I meet young people whose disappointment with the church has turned into outright disgust.[5]

But, thank God, the church is making a strong beginning to rectify this intolerable situation. The church is getting into the forefront of the action. The blood which has been spilled in these past years has been mingled with the blood of those Christians who have dared to involve their very safety in the struggle.

III. Sensitivity to God's Moral Constraints

Then, finally, this pithy parable underscores the fact that, sometimes, those "outside" are more sensitive to God than those "inside." It is obvious that when Jonah finally relented and decided to go to Nineveh, he rather relished the thought of preaching God's judgment on that ancient and implacable enemy of the Jews. He hated those marauding bands which had roved the Jewish hillsides, raiding their villages and murdering the people. So he walked the streets of Nineveh knowing that the people would not respond. Yet, totally in contradiction to every preconceived notion he had, when the people of Nineveh heard the message of the prophet, they repented—every last soul!

Surely our insensitivity is not enough to let us miss this point; it should stab the conscience of the Christian church broad awake. Many who are most sensitive to the hurt and agony of modern life, who are most conscious of the social inequities, and who are struggling with the structures of our common life to wrest from them meaning for every human being are not Christian in any overt sense of the word. In

---

5. Martin Luther King, Jr., "Letter from Birmingham Jail," *The Christian Century*, June 12, 1963, pp. 767–73.

government, in industry, in labor, in management, in politics, there are countless people who are fighting to eradicate the social ills of our society and who are not Christian. At the same time, in government, in industry, in labor, in management, in politics, there are Christians who oppose all social action programs. In fact, they have joined hands in scuttling some of the most progressive and humanitarian legislation ever proposed in the history of the United States.

Within a church I served this was the case. Some young men who were in VISTA (Volunteers In Service To America) came to me in 1967 to ask for a small room within our church building for a meeting place where they could teach basic skills in reading, writing, arithmetic, and daily living to a group of impoverished, educationally deprived people of the county. These two young men were involved, secularly, in service to a deprived and needy people. The deacons, the elected leadership in a Baptist church, turned their request down and refused to make such space available. Those "outside" the institutional church were more sensitive to human need than those "inside."

I think of Albert Camus, the novelist who was the recipient of the Nobel Prize for Literature in 1957. He found it impossible to reconcile the existence of God and human responsibility; therefore, he was an unbeliever, an iconoclast and, yet, a sensitive soul who illuminated the problems of the human conscience. Here was a man "outside" the institutional church; but, at the same time, this sensitive soul vigorously and passionately repudiated capital punishment. At the same time there are Christians who defend this medieval, antiquarian practice called capital punishment. In condoning it, they are denying a fundamental affirmation of their theology, namely, the inherent worth of all human life. Here was a man "outside" the church who was more sensitive to life's agonies than some who are "inside" the church.

I think of Harry Golden, who is editor and publisher of the *North Carolina Israelite*. The causes he has championed across the years indicate that he is a sensitive soul. For example, the fact that he had condemned segregation as inherently evil for years previous to 1954 illumines and amplifies my contention that some "outsiders" are more sensitive than "insiders." At the precise time Harry Golden was struggling for civil rights in eloquent and prophetic terms, much of the Christian church was advocating a stance of noninvolvement by either silence or condemnation of those involved in the civil rights sit-ins and kneel-ins. In effect, such a stance was a defense of the status quo wherein the most segregated hour of the week is still the eleven o'clock worship hour. Now, I ask, who is the most sensitive to the human struggle?

But, there is another side to it. Even though there are countless people "outside" the church who are agonizing and struggling with evil, there is an awakening "inside" the church. Even though I grow impatient waiting on my own denomination to arouse sufficiently, I am elated by evidence that it is definitely beginning to move into the structures of the secular life to redeem them. Christians are awakening to the fact that God is served wherever we are involved in the demand for justice, in the crucial issues of progressive legislation, in the civil rights movements, in the struggle for world peace.

I illustrate by repeating a story which James Armstrong told of a visit he had with Dr. S. P. Raju in Hyderabad, India. Dr. Raju, an engineer and scientist, invented the smokeless oven which is so prominent in India's villages. He designed a one-room house that is intended to improve the living conditions of the peasants of the country. He is an official in the Indian government. He is also a remarkable Christian. He has one of the most sensitive Christian consciences imaginable. He views his ministry in the honored tradition of servanthood. His paraphrase of some of Paul's words expresses his commitment.

Raju, a servant of Jesus Christ, called to be an engineer, separated unto the Gospel of God in the evangelism of irrigation research for growing more food and bringing redemption from hunger. . . . Also separated unto the Gospel of God in the evangelism of housing research for the poor, for bringing "preventive redemption" to them from congestion, dirt and disease, which are the potential sources of moral evil and sin.

Here is the kind of sensitivity of spirit for which Jonah is contending as a quickening word of God.

So the live word of God is that God's love is indefatigable. And the tragic figure of Jonah around whom this parable is woven represents a harsh, intolerant spirit which stands over against the eternity of God's universal love. The broad sweep of that universal love comes surging out of the prophetic burden of Jonah to underscore the fact that the shallow levels of an intolerant spirit must be deepened to whatever depth is required in order that the creative love of God may flow for the healing of the hurts and pangs of a creation alienated and estranged from its creator.

261.8   Sanders, Robert
S

Radical Voices in the Wilderness

261.8   Sanders, Robert
S

Radical Voices in the Wilderness